Trailar
Ana
Shankari Mataji

ISBN-13: 978-1499166583
ISBN-10: 1499166583

First Published by:
Shrimat Swami Paramananda Saraswati
"Bhajan Ashram"
142, Ayudhgarbi (Near Harish Chandra Ghat Road)
The Holy KASHI DHAM
(P.O. Varanasi) UP.
1357 Bengali

Published for the second time by:
Amar Nath Poddar
Ex-President & Trustee
Shri Guru Ashram Trailanga Math
35/24 Biddyatan Sarani
Kolkata 700035

Mahayogeshwar Trailanga Swami

Shankari Mataji

Contents

Prologue

Many in the West are aware of the great sages of India – Mahatma Trailanga Swami and his direct disciple, the great woman ascetic Shankari Mataji. But unfortunately not much information is available on the lives of these august personages. This book is our humble attempt to shed some light on these extraordinary lives.

This biography is an English translation of a Bengali book written by the direct disciple of Shankari Mataji, Swami Paramananda Saraswati. Published in 1949, this book contains facts about the great Swami narrated by Shankari Mataji herself to the author.

The author, whose birth name was Paresh Dasgupta, was born on February 7, 1889 at Dacca (now Bangladesh). A doctor by profession, he first met Mataji at Darjeeling in July 1931, and was later initiated by her in Novenber 1932 at Kaccha and renamed 'Paramanda Saraswati'. He became a *sanyasi* and had the rare fortune of spending 18 years at the holy feet of Mataji, right until her *Mahasamadhi* on March 1, 1949. Seated in the yogic posture, she consciously left her body at 12:30 am at her own residence "Bhajan Ashram" in Kashi. She was 122 years old at the time.

This book was published three months after her Samadhi in June 1949.

Swami Paramananda left this earthly abode in 1956.

How the publisher discovered this extremely rare book, and a few other works and interesting facts with it, makes for an engaging read.

Publisher's note

The book on Maha Yogeshwar Baba Shri Trailanga Swami & His disciple Shri Shri Shankari Mataji`s life histories could not have been published as a new edition without the blessings of both. The following facts clearly prove that their blessings were bestowed on us.

The publisher was the President of Shri Guru Ashram Trailanga Math of Baranagore in 2005. All of sudden, he got an invitation from the Board of Trustees of the Dakshineshwar Debottor Estate to speak on the life of Mahaguru Shri Trailanga Swami. This program was scheduled to be held at Dakshineshwar, where Shri Ramakrishna Paramahamsa Deva used to meet with various *sadhakas* & saints at different times, near the historical Panchawati & Jhawbon. This is the place where a new *Dhyan Bhavan* (meditation room) has been constructed by the temple authorities.

However, the publisher was compelled to convey with deep regret that he was unable to speak on the life, ideology, and teachings of the great yogi. He also felt that he was utterly unfit to be the President of the *Math*. From that moment onwards, he resolved to spend his energies in finding out more about the life and teachings of the great yogi. However, to honor the invitation, he requested other members of the *Math* to attend the program at Dakshineshwar and speak on the life of the Mahaguru. But they also expressed their inability to speak.

At that moment the honor of the *Math* was somehow saved when two people, who were not our members of the *Math*, spoke on our behalf.

Due to the deep sense of guilt and shame that he felt at this episode, and with the grace and blessings ofMahaguru Trailanga Swami, the publisher embarked on a new direction.

From that time onwards, he engaged himself like a man obsessed, regularly contacting various ashrams that were following the Mahaguru's systems and teachings, and scouring for more details on his life by collecting and reading old books, valuable data and information from various libraries, the Internet, old book shops, and talking to many elderly devotees, and going to various places including British Library & Museum.

During the process of collecting all this invaluable information and contacting many wise and divine personalities, gradually, by the grace of the Mahaguru, amazing incidents happened to him. At that time, the publisher could not foresee how, through an astounding sequence of events, he would become acquainted with Shri Kulandai Ganeshan Swamiji, living in the village of Batla Gundu near Madurai, so far away from Kolkata. Ganeshan Swamiji happened to manage and administer the *Samadhi Mandir* of the mother of the Mahaguru. In doing so, he had been also following the directive of his late grandfather, Raghupathi Venkata Raghavan Swami (who was also a disciple of the Mahaguru), and had been conducting research for the last 30 years in an attempt to put together a comprehensive history of the life of Trailanga Swamiji and publish it.

Then the publisher was fortunate to connect with the Paramananda Yogananda Yogashram situated in Halisahar Town in the North 24 Parganas District of West Bengal. This Yogashram was established by Shri Yogananda Swami who was a disciple of Shri Paramananda Swami (nephew of Shri Trailanga Swamiji) and who had the good fortune to meet Trailanga Swamiji on two occasions. He took *samadhi* in 1975.

And likewise, he was fortunate to come in touch with the Swami Bag Ashram (originally in Dhaka, Bangla Desh and now relocated to Sodepure, North 24 Parganas) which was established by Shri Tripuralinga Saraswati, the fifth disciple of the Mahaguru. This is where the auspicious birth anniversary of Shri Trailanga Swami is still observed with reverence.

The publisher also felt very fortunate that he was able to collect biographical narratives of disciples of the Mahaguru, which were previously unpublished. Most noteworthy among them were narratives on the complete life of Shri Tripuralinga Saraswati, Swamji`s *Manasa Putri* Shri Shankari Mataji's biography and a short biography by the Bengali disciple Shri Umacharan Mukhopadhay.

During this period of collecting material, by the grace of Swamiji, the publisher could visit the Bhajan Ashram of Shri Shri Shankari Mataji in Varanasi Dham in 2007—after attending the birth day celebrations of Swamiji in his *ashram* at Pancha Ganga Ghat Varanasi. After paying his respects and making offerings at various *maths*, *ashrams* and temples in Varanasi, and after a long search, he reached Bhajan Ashram of Shri Shri Shankari Mataji at Audhgarbi near Harish Chandra Ghat. When the writer knocked at the main gate, a very old woman came out and in response to his question, confirmed that this house indeed was the Bhajan Ashram of Mataji. They were residing there after purchasing the house. She also very generously made an offer in Hindi: "*Agar Tum Dekhna Chahate Ho Matajika Puja Ghar Dekh Sekto Ho.*" (If you wish to see Mataji`s worship room you may do so). Accepting her offer eagerly, the publisher entered the house associated with the memories of Shri Shri Mataji. He sat in the worship room of Mataji and was astonished to find that members of this non-Bengali family were still worshiping twice a day the idols of Radharaman, the Mahaguru and other gods & goddesses, and a *Shivalinga*—all of which were installed by Mataji. And a stone idol of Shri Shri Mataji was also installed there by her disciples after her *samadhi*.

After spending sometime in the holy room, the writer asked the kind lady if they had ever found any item used by Shri Mataji, or any diaries, letters, papers, books etc. She replied in Hindi: "*Beta Bohut Kuch Tha, Lekin Humlog Bengali Nahi Samajhte, Isliye Sab Kuch Gangajime Ger Diya. Lekin Unka Teen Kitab Abhi Tak Hai. Tumhe Chahe To Le Sakte Ho.*" (My son, there were many things, but we don't understand Bengali and so we immersed all of it in the Ganga. However three books are still lying. If you want, you may take them). Then she gave me 3 books from a very old tin box. One of them was published in 1949, and was Shri Shri Mataji`s dictated notes written down by her disciple Swami Paramananda; which turned to be invaluable material on the lives of the Mahaguru and his disciple.Upon the request of many devotees and friends, I have taken the opportunity to reprint this holy book for the devotees of the Mahaguru & Shri Shri Shankari Mataji on a non-commercial basis as a part of my *Guru Puja*.

Considering this as a blessing of the Mahaguru, the publisher touched the books to his forehead in obeisance to them. After expressing heartfelt gratitude and paying his respects to the old lady and other family members, the publisher left the holy place.

A few days after returning to Calcutta, he tried to read the books and found that they were quite damaged due to ordinary storage for such a long period of time. Then he attempted again to read, this time handling the manuscript on the lives of the Mahaguru and his disciple Shri Shri Shankari Mataji with extreme caution.

He was overwhelmed on discovering many astonishing facts that were till then unknown and unpublished.

Especially noteworthy among them was the description of the meeting of the Mahaguru with Shri Ramakrishna Paramahamsa in 1869 and Thakur

Ramkrishnadev's four questions posed to the Mahaguru and his answers. Another interesting detail was that a *Gurumata* to Ramakrishnadev, Yogini Bhairavi Ma, was, in fact, a disciple of the Mahaguru. This fact was unknown to all, along with the detail that it was on the explicit orders of the Mahaguru that Bhairavi Maa went to Dakshineshwar to clear all obstacles in the *Tantric Sadhana Path* of Shri Ramakrishnadev.

By the grace and blessings of both the great yogi and yogini, when seeking the whereabouts of another living disciple of Shri Shri Shankari Mataji, he reached Srimati Basanti Choudhury`s house as well, where he found a *Namaboli* (a scarf with the names of deities printed on it) used by Shri Shri Shankari Mataji. In the book "Maha Yogini Chira Kumari Sanyasini Shri Shri Shankari Mataji" published by Shri Jagat Jyoti Choudhary, the able son of Srimati Basanti Choudhary, there is a description of how the latter became Shri Shri Shankari Mataji's disciple in the last portion of the book.

Most Humbly,
Baba's lowly Servant,
Shri Amar Nath Poddar
Ex-President & Member of the Trustee board
Shri Guru Ashram Trailanga Math
Kolkata 700035
06.11.2011

Foreword

Yogini Mother Shri Shankari Mataji, a direct disciple of Maha Yogeswar Swami Trailanga, the living Bhagavan Shankara, is the most illustrious and remarkable woman saint the world has seen. The enchanting and exemplary biography of Her Holiness is an extension of the *Mahacharitra* of Maha Swami Trailanga, and an excellent model for aspiring ascetics. Among the sentient, man occupies the foremost place, and among men, the ascetic saint is the nearest approximation to the original substance God, who reveals Himself best in the heart of the saint. Divinity, in all its excellence, shines in the saint. Having this in mind and to show that a woman can also be a great model of renunciation and asceticism, untainted by the world of illusion, the Maha Swami, through his *sankalpa*, conceived an ascetic female child (*manasaputri*) and brought her to this phenomenal world.

He selected His foremost, elderly, and lifelong ascetic disciple Kalikananda Swami as the girl's father and Shrimati Rajalakshmi Devi, an ardent young lady devotee and *Shivabhakta Shiromani*, ambitious to become a monk, as her mother. This strange unification by the Mahaswami of a young *brahmacharini* mother and an old *sanyasin* father, in *Grihastashrama Dharma*, resulted in the birth of a female child. One can never see such a divine and blessed family, wherein all the three—father, mother, and daughter—are saints,*sanyasins* and, direct disciples of Mahatma Trailanga Swami.

It is worth noting that Maha Swamiji's birth, upbringing and spiritual life are truly reflected in Shankari Ma. As a child, the Maha Swami was left at the Lotus Feet of Mother Goddess (by his parents selected by the Goddess), who brought Him up in their own sanctum sanctorum and made him a very great Shiva yogi of the Himalayan pattern. Likewise, Shankari Ma, as a child, was left under His (Trailanga's) care. Her upbringing and tutelage were under His direct supervision in His own inner sanctum at His ashram, and she was later sent to the Himalayas to perfect herself as a great yogini.

Verily, Ma Shankari appears as a true female Shakti form of Swami Trailanga, resembling Him in most of His divine aspects. Her long penance, silent, secluded and sincere *sadhana* away from the madding crowds, extensive spiritual entourages, ever-flowing spiritual dynamism, all-encompassing motherly affection, are a few of the similarities of note with the Mahaguru. As and when the Maha Swami desired for the sake of His devotees, the cosmic Mother readily appeared in person to give Him *darshan*—even from images of *Devatas*.

The compassionate Mahaguru granted a special boon to Shankari Ma—as and when and wherever she wanted, He would at once appear before her to attend to her needs. Such was the unique position Shankari Ma held in the mind of the great Mahaguru. He created her in the physical form of the Bala Kali Mata—called Mangala Gowri—installed by Him in His ashram. At the age of eight, Shankari Ma was carried deep into the sacred waters of the Ganga on His shoulders and shown the living form of Mahashakti Maha Kali—as an eight-year-old girl resembling Shankari Ma.

Nearly 46 years later, another chosen disciple, Shri Umacharan, also had a face-to-face *darshan* of Bala Kali Mata by the grace of Mahaguru. To this child of Swami Trailanga, her Guru was everything—*Mata*, *Pita*, Guru, and *Devata*.

During her early childhood, Shankari worshiped a wooden idol of Lord Ramachandra, her *Kuladevata*. One day, she thought of worshiping her Guru Trailanga, living in the next house. And when started moving out to do so, she heard the sweet divine voice of her Mahaguru telling her, "Why are you troubling yourself, my child? I am here to accept your *puja*."

Surprised, Shankari stepped into the *puja* room to see her beloved Mahaguru sitting on the pedestal where Lord Ramachandra's idol was kept. Swimming in the loving grace, she was convinced that the Mahaguru was also her God and *Kuladevata*, Lord Ramachandra.

The divine design of Swami Trailanga was most appropriate. He ensured Shankari was born on Rama Navami, the birthday of her *Kuladevata*. The birth star of Shankari was *Pushya*, the same as her Mahaguru. He imparted rigorous training to the 12 year old with the observance of *Brahmacharya Vrata* for 12 years in complete seclusion. No ordinary girl could have borne the brunt of such strict discipline for such a long duration. What an extraordinary and exemplary Guru and an equally extraordinary and exemplary *shishya*!

Another unique aspect of this relationship was that during the period of study and *sadhana*, both rarely met and the Mahaguru was even away from Varanasi at times. How then did Shankari excel? Mahaswami simply thought and Shankari got it all instantly. The above incidents are being recalled to highlight and impress upon the readers the greatness of both, who are truly towering spiritual personalities.

Both stoutly kept away from public gaze. The Mahaguru stressed that the shackles of publicity are an obstacle to the quiet ministry of spirituality and a hindrance to the vow of renunciation. Ma Shankari was every inch the prototype of her Master. Probably because of these views, the concept of publicity was abhorrent to their disciples and hence very little attempt was made to record and publish this vital information about these two great saints having an exceptionally long history of over three centuries.

Certainly Umacharan attempted and was successful in the publication of the biography of Mahaswami based on hearsay and documentation of his own experiences and *upadesa* (received directly from the Mahaswami) nearly two decades after the *Mahasamadhi* of Mahaswami. But there is no mention about the most illustrious direct disciple and *manasaputri* Shri Shankari Mata in Shri Umacharan's biography. All the other biographies of Swami Trailanga are of commercial nature, blindly reproducing Umacharan's writings and they don't mention anything about the great Shankari Ma, who was a resident of Benares till 1950. Even the recent editions of the biographies of Mahaswami in Bengali and Hindi were found incomplete as they failed to include the enchanting history of Shankari Ma.

Contrary to such negligence, we, the devotees and descendants of Shri Mahaswami from south, especially in the native village of Mahaswami, are proud to place on record that the great yogini Shankari Ma finds a place in the sanctum sanctorum of the Mahaswami temple at Batlagundu village. Information collected and verified for over 30 years from Varanasi during our several visits to the holy place, which proudly enshrines the Bhajan Ashram of Her Holiness Shankari Ma, and a short biography of Her, has been included in our enlarged edition of Mahaswami's *Mahacharitra* in Tamil called 'Guru Darshan-3', which is now being rendered in both English and Bengali.

The benign grace of Mahaguru has found a sincere and devoted associate in this noble task of rendering the details of the biography of Shankari Ma in Shri Amarnath Poddar, a true devotee of Mahaswami, and an active member of the trust board of Guru Ashram Trailanga Math,

Kolkata, without whose selfless efforts, this project would not have been successful.

As a young brother, he has taken pains to collect the books on Mahaswami and Shankari Ma and information from the internet and other sources and arranged to render them into English for our onward publication in Tamil. We, the grand children of Mahaswami from Tamil Nadu, will also enjoy the nectar of the biography of our beloved Shankari Ma by the untiring efforts of our brother disciple Shri Amarnath Poddar in rendering the book in English, with the sincere, ephemeral and industrious editing work of Shri Dinesh N. based in California, a dedicated devotee of Mahaswami, who voluntarily came forward to bring out the English version of the Bengali book.

His earnestness and dedication shows that he is blessed to be an instrument in the hands of our Mahaguru Bhagavan Trailanga Swami Maharaj.

With the divine guidance of Mahaguru, Shri Poddar has now arranged to bring out a reprint of the only Bengali book on Trailanga Swami and Shankari Ma by Swami Paramananda Saraswati, a direct disciple of Shankari Ma for the sake of the true devotees. This book as such is a sweet divine gift of Maha Swami to His beloved children of Bengal, as bliss and blessings are beyond the purview of commercial exploitation.

This foreword, in addition, stresses the fact in the words of Swami Binoyananda Giri, a Kriyayogi, that "Shankari Ma in my opinion is not a follower of Bhakti yoga, but is trying to solve the problem of life through complete surrender of the self to the Guru, not blindly, but with a rationalistic analysis of the problem of our lives in its various aspects, believing that religion is an individual problem."

It is most significant to bring it to the notice of all that Shankari Mata was present during the meeting of Shri Ramakrishna Paramahamsa with Swami Trailanga in 1869. It is only she, an enlightened being, that was able to give to the world the most important four '*upadesas*' that Maha Swami gave to Sri Ramakrishnadev, which formed the basis of the spiritual experiences (*sadhana*) of Shri Ramakrishna and subsequently helped Swami Vivekananda in the establishment of the Ramakrishna Math and Mission.

On this happy occasion of the celebration of *Maha Pooja*, we deem it as a fitting offering to the Master Trailanga Swami and Mother Shankari Ma and to the people, the Vedanta as lived by Her Holiness Shri Shri Sankari Mata.

To study, ponder over and understand her is verily *Brahma Vidya*.

With this attitude of dedication, this book is released.

KulandaiSwami Ganesan
"Shri Kulandai Vilasam"
Shri Trilinga Swami Temple
Old No: 9-6-20, New No: 9-6-37
Single Street, Agraharam,
Batlagundu P.O - 624202,
Dindigul District, Tamil Nadu

শ্রীমৎ স্বামী পরমানন্দ সরস্বতী ও গুরুমাতা আবাল্য সন্ন্যাসিনী
শ্রীশ্রীশঙ্করী মা
(শেষদিনকার ১২৩ বছরের, চারতালা ছাদে মধ্যাহ্ন কালীন
ফটো ২৮-২-১৯৫৩)

This photograph of Shankari Mata and Paramanand Saraswati was taken on the rooftop of Bhajan Ashram on the last day of her life on earth by Swami Raman Giri.

Preface[1]

Our venerable Guru-Mata Shri Shri Shankari Mataji lived 61 years of her life in the holy proximity of His Holiness, the world famous Trailanga Swami, as an ashramite. She was brought up and had received *deeksha* (initiation) and spiritual instruction from the great teacher. The saint, who had undertaken a *Mouna Vrata* (vow of silence), would break his silence once a week in order to give spiritual guidance to his disciples, in the same room where he practiced devotional austerities (*sadhana*). This book is based on the stories of his life, as narrated by Trailanga Swami, in response to questions from his disciples. Mataji in turn narrated it to us afterward, and also shared those experiences and insights gained by her during her long stay with her world famous Guru.

Our humble intention behind this publication is to convey the holy messages from the Maha Sanyasi of our modern times, and offer our salutations to him.

Astute readers might notice that Mataji avoided narrating any mundane details of the great teacher's life, and instead focused only on the aspects she felt as being essential, as well as the aspects that conveyed the divinity of the great Teacher and would help in the upliftment of masses. She told us the way he practised austerities, the yoga, to detach one-self from matters mundane and progress towards the eventual liberation of the soul. Her Holiness, our Mataji, wished us all to be aware of the divine life of Trailanga Swami and its significance.

We must confess here that this book lacks perfect coherence, and thus may not do full justice in reflecting the great sage's entire life and messages.

However, we vow to re-organise the text of this book to perfection so far possible in the second part of this book.

We pray to the Almighty, His Holiness Shri Trailanga Swami, and our Guru-Mother Her Holiness Shri Shri Mataji to grace and bless our humble undertaking.

The author would like to express his gratitude to the respected professor Shri Priyaranjan Sen, M.A., P.H.S. and our respected religious brother,

---

[1] What follows from here is English translation of the original Bangali manuscript

devout man, professor Shri Ramada Prasanna Ghosh, M.A., who toiled hard to make this publication possible in reality, along with some other devout souls.

Devoted Servant to the feet of Shri Shri Mataji
"Dean Paramananda"
1949

Mangalaacharanam

ब्रह्मानन्दं परमसुखदं केवलं ज्ञानमुर्तिं

द्वन्द्वातीतं गगनसदृशं तत्त्वमस्यादिलक्ष्यम्।

एकं नित्यं विमलमचलं सर्वधीसाक्षिभूतं

भावातीतं त्रिगुणरहितं सद्गुरुं तम् नमामि॥ १॥

brahmānandaṁ paramasukhadaṁ kevalaṁ ñānamurtiṁ
dvandvāatītaṁ gaganasadṛśaṁ tattvamasyādilakṣyam |
ekaṁ nityaṁ vimalacalaṁ sarvadhīsākṣibhūtaṁ
bhāvātītaṁ triguṇarahitaṁ sadguruṁ taṁ namāmi || 1 ||

चिद्रूपेन परिव्यात्पम् त्रैलोक्यम् सचराचरम्।

तत्पदं दर्शितं येन तस्मै श्री गुरवे नमः॥२॥

cidrupena parivyātpam trailokyam sacarācaram |
tatpadaṁ darśitaṁ yena tasmai śrī gurave namaḥ || 2 ||

र्वश्रुतिशिरोरत्नविराजितपदाम्बुजः।

वेदान्ताम्बुजसूर्यो यस्तस्मै श्रीगुरवे नमः॥३॥

sarvaśrutiśiroratnavirājitapadāmbujaḥ |
vedāntāmbujasūryo yastasmai śrīgurave namaḥ || 3 ||

चैतन्यं शाश्वतं शान्तं व्योमातितं निरञ्जनम्।

नाद्बिन्दुकलात्तीतं तस्मै श्रीगुरवे नमः॥ ४॥

caitanyaṁ śāśvataṁ śāntaṁ vyomātitaṁ nirañjanam |
nādbindukalāttītaṁ tasmai śrīgurave namaḥ || 4 ||

ज्ञानशक्तिसमारुढस्तत्त्वमाला विभूषितः।

भुक्तिमुक्तिप्रदाता यस्तस्मै श्रीगुरवे नमः॥ ५॥

ñānaśaktisamāruḍhastattvamālā vibhūṣitaḥ |
bhuktimuktipradātā yastasmai śrīgurave namaḥ || 5 ||

अनेकजन्मसम्प्राप्तसर्वकर्मविदाहिने।

स्वात्मज्ञानप्रभावेण तस्मै श्रीगुरवे नमः॥ ६॥

anekajanmasamprāptasarvakarmavidāhine |
svātmañānaprabhāveṇa tasmai śrīgurave namaḥ || 6 ||

शोषणं भवसिन्धोश्च ज्ञापनं सारसम्पदः।

गुरोः पादोदकं सम्यक् तस्मै श्रीगुरवे नमः॥ ७॥

śoṣaṇaṁ bhavasindhośca ñāpanaṁ sārasampadaḥ |
guroḥ pādodakaṁ samyak tasmai śrīgurave namaḥ || 7 ||

न गुरोरधिकं तत्वं न गुरोरधिकं तपः।

तत्वज्ञानात् परं नास्ति तस्मै श्रीगुरवे नमः॥ ८॥

na guroradhikaṁ tatvaṁ na guroradhikaṁ tapaḥ |
tatvañānāt paraṁ nāsti tasmai śrīgurave namaḥ || 8 ||

गुरुरादिरनादिश्च गुरुः परमदैवतम्।

गुरोः परतरं नास्ति तस्मै श्रीगुरवे नमः॥ ९॥

gururādiranādiśca guruḥ paramadaivatam |
guroḥ parataraṁ nāsti tasmai śrīgurave namaḥ || 9 ||

मन्नाथः श्रीजगन्नाथः मद्गुरुः श्रीजगद्गुरुः।

मदात्मा सर्वभूतात्मा तस्मै श्रीगुरवे नमः॥ १०॥

mannāthaḥ śrījagannāthaḥ madguruḥ śrījagadguruḥ |
madātmā sarvabhūtātmā tasmai śrīgurave namaḥ || 10 ||

Shri Shri Trailangastakam

श्री श्री त्रैलिंगाष्टकम्

śrī śrī trailiṁgāṣṭakam

वन्दे देवं जंगमतीर्थं यतिराजं

सौम्यं शान्तं दान्तमशेष-शशिवदनं।

शुद्धं बुद्धं मुक्तमनष्टं भगवन्तं

श्री त्रैलिंगं ख्यात-विवेकं शिवारामं॥ १॥

vande devaṁ jaṁgama-tīrthaṁ yatirājaṁ
saumyaṁ śāntaṁ dāntamaśeṣa-śaśi-vadanaṁ |
śuddhaṁ buddhaṁ muktamanaṣṭaṁ bhagavantaṁ
śrī trailiṁgaṁ khyāta-vivekaṁ śivārāmaṁ || 1 ||

भीमं कान्तं नग्न-मुण्डं चिरसुस्थं

प्राणारामं श्यामलकान्तिं सुविशालं।

ज्योतिपुंजं योगविलासं गुणावासं

श्री त्रैलिंगं पुण्यनिकुंजं विमलांगं॥ २॥

bhīmaṁ kāntaṁ nagna-muṇḍaṁ cira-susthaṁ
prāṇārāmaṁ śyāmala-kāntiṁ suviśālaṁ |
jyotipuṁjaṁ yoga-vilāsaṁ guṇāvāsaṁ
śrī trailiṁgaṁ puṇya-nikuṁjaṁ vimalāṁgaṁ || 2 ||

नाना-शास्त्रैः वेदकथनैर्वा अलब्धं

स्वस्थं धीरं भावगभीरं वरेण्यं।

शुद्धं शान्तं जन्मविविक्तं गतमायं

श्री त्रैलिंगं मूर्तविरागं शुचिशीलं॥ ३ ॥

nānā-śāstraiḥ veda-kathanairvā alabdhaṁ
svasthaṁ dhīraṁ bhāva-gabhīraṁ vareṇyaṁ |
śuddhaṁ śāntaṁ janma-viviktaṁ gatamāyaṁ
śrī trailiṁgaṁ mūrta-virāgaṁ śuci-śīlaṁ || 3 ||

भावाभाव-प्रत्यहीनं गृह-शून्यं

द्वन्द्वातीतं पूर्णमनीहं निरपांगं।

नित्यानन्दं प्रेम-विहगं सम-चित्तं

श्री त्रैलिंगं त्यक्त-विकल्पं शिवकल्पं॥ ४ ॥

bhāvābhāva-pratyahīnaṁ gṛha-śūnyaṁ
dvandvātītaṁ pūrṇamanīhaṁ nirapāṁgaṁ |
nityānandaṁ prema-vihagaṁ sama-cittaṁ
śrī trailiṁgaṁ tyakta-vikalpaṁ śiva-kalpaṁ || 4 ||

जीवन्मुक्तं ध्यान-नियुक्तं गुणमुक्तं

मायातीतं मनोविहीनं जन्मानन्यं।

ब्रह्मानन्दं सुशित-बुद्धिं धृति-मौनं

श्री त्रैलिंगं दीनदयार्द्रं शिवारामं॥ ५॥

jīvanmuktaṁ dhyāna-niyuktaṁ guṇamuktaṁ
māyātītaṁ manovihīnaṁ janmānanyaṁ |
brahmānandaṁ suśita-buddhiṁ dhṛti-maunaṁ
śrī trailiṁgaṁ dīna-dayārdraṁ śivārāmaṁ || 5 ||

सत्याभीष्टं ज्ञानगरिष्ठं गत-मोहनं

स्वेच्छामृत्युं निर्मज्जित-कामं नतवामं।

गंगानन्दं मंगळाखन्डं सुकुमारं

श्री त्रैलिंगं कीर्ति-किरीटं कलिभीष्मं ॥ ६ ॥

satyābhīṣṭaṁ jñāna-gariṣṭhaṁ gata-mohanaṁ
svecchā-mṛtyuṁ nirmajjita-kāmaṁ nata-vāmaṁ |
gaṁgānandaṁ maṁgaḻākhanḍaṁ sukumāraṁ
śrī trailiṁgaṁ kīrti-kirīṭaṁ kali-bhīṣmaṁ || 6 ||

वाराणस्यां लोक-हितार्थं निवसन्तं

संख्यातीतैर्-भक्त-समूहैः शत-वर्षं।

नित्य-भक्ति-पूजित-पादाम्बु-युग्मं

श्री त्रैलिंगं तपस्-सूर्यं नापवर्ज्यं ॥ ७ ॥

vārāṇasyāṁ loka-hitārthaṁ nivasantaṁ
saṁkhyātītair-bhakta-samūhaiḥ śata-varṣaṁ |
nitya-bhakti-pūjita-pādāmbu-yugmaṁ
śrī trailiṁgaṁ tapas-sūryaṁ nāpavarjyaṁ || 7 ||

यो वा जन्तोस्-त्वन्तिमानं गम्य-मानं

माया-शक्तं तपश्शक्तं शूलि-मन्यं।

लोकानां नो लौकिक-मनैर्-अभिगम्यं

वन्दे देवं मूर्त-महेशं भजनीयं ॥ ८ ॥

yo vā jantos-tvantimānaṁ gamya-mānaṁ
māyā-śaktaṁ tapaśśaktaṁ śūli-manyaṁ|
lokānāṁ no laukika-manair-abhigamyaṁ
vande devaṁ mūrta-maheśaṁ bhajanīyaṁ || 8 ||

भक्ति-श्रद्धा-भाव-समेतैः पठनीयं

स्तोत्रं पुण्यं ज्ञान-निधनं जन-वृन्दैः।

ध्यात्वा ध्याता पातक-दोषात् दुःख-मुक्तः

सद्यो गच्छेद्-अभियोगे शिव-लोकम्॥

bhakti-śraddhā-bhāva-sametaiḥ paṭhanīyaṁ
stotraṁ puṇyaṁ jñāna-nidhanaṁ jana-vṛndaiḥ |
dhyātvā dhyātā pātaka-doṣāt duḥkha-muktaḥ
sadyo gacched-abhiyoge śiva-lokam ||

॥ ॐ तत् सत्॥

॥ ॐ नमो गणेशाय नमः॥

|| om tat sat ||
|| om namo gaṇeśāya namaḥ ||

नारायणं नमस्कृत्य नरं चैव नरोत्तमम्।

देवीं सरस्वतीं चैव ततो जयमुदीरयेत्॥

nārāyaṇaṁ namaskṛtya naraṁ caiva narottamam |
devīṁ sarasvatīṁ caiva tato jayamudīrayet ||

Introduction

India, our great motherland, has been the abode of spiritualism since ages. Here, the majesty of *Sanatana Dharma* is reflected everywhere by the grace of the Almighty, the Creator of the universe. It is indeed spiritualism that has been the spine of our nation and social life since time immemorial. In this holy land, we take the name of the good Lord in every step of our daily life; it's a place where beggars seek alms by singing the glories of the Divine and many perspire to serve the purpose of God.

It is evident from our history that whenever sin and irreligiousness predominate, avatars and great religious teachers descend to demolish all the inauspiciousness, and re-establish religious sanctity.

यदा यदा हि धर्मस्य ग्लानिर्भवति भारत।

अभ्युत्थानमधर्मस्य तदात्मानं स्रजाय्महम्॥

परित्राणाय साधुनां विनाशाय च दुष्क्रताम्।

धर्मसंस्थापनार्थाय सम्भवामि युगे युगे॥

yadā yadā hi dharmasya glānirbhavati bhārata |
abhyutthānam adharmasya tadātmānang srijāmyaham ||
paritrāyāyna sādhunāng vināśāya cha dushkritām |
dharma sangsthāpanārthāya sambhavāani yuge yuge ||

(The Bhagavad Gita – 4:8)

Translation

Whenever there is decay of righteousness, O Bharata, and exaltation of unrighteousness, then do I create myself, I incarnate myself in some form. For the protection of the good, and the destruction of evil-doers, for the sake of firmly establishing righteousness, I am born from age to age.

इत्थं यदा यदा बाधा दानवोत्था भविष्यति॥

तदा तदावतीर्याहं करिष्याम्यरिसंक्षयम्॥

itthaṁ yadā yadā bādhā danavotthā bhaviṣyati ||
tadā tadāvatīryāhaṁ kariṣyāmyarisaṁkṣayam ||

(Shri Durga Saptashati – 11:54)

Translation

Thus whenever trouble arises due to the advent of the danavas, I shall incarnate and destroy the foes, and
ensure peace, piousness, and sanctity of life.

जब जब हो धरम कि हानि । बढे अधर्म असुर अभिमानी ।

तब तब प्रभु धरि विविध शरिरा । हरहिन क्रिपानिधि सज्जन पीडा।

jaba jaba ho dharama hi hāni | baḍhe adharma asura abhimanī |
taba taba prabhu dhari vividha śarirā | harahina kripanidhi sajjana pīḍā |

(Bal Kanda / Ramcharitmanas by Tulsidas)

Translation

Whenever there is impurity of religion and unspeakable injustice and oppression from the demonical powers, and when the Brahmins, cows, devatas and Mother Earth suffer a lot, then the blissful Almighty incarnates to deliver respite to them from the injustice and the suffering.

Innumerable times in our history, whenever the dark clouds of falsehood cover the light of truth, and when common people suffer from various miseries that ail the world and are seeking freedom from such a state, there is inevitably the advent of saints on earth, carrying the torch of Truth and Spirituality, to liberate souls from the dungeon of impurity and ignorance.

In this manner, time and again, avatars or spiritual gurus came with their supreme knowledge and taught devotion, self-restraint, love, compassion, and spiritual activities for the welfare of the masses, and thus saved the people of India. That is the glorious history of our land through the ages.

The paths towards the betterment of humanity, as adviced by these demi-gods and preceptors, are the true avenues to walk on, and in that way the people suffering from *tritap* (anguish of three sorts)—(a) physical and mental; (b) coming from creatures; and, (c) natural or divine—could get the much-needed respite. It is wise to follow the footsteps of these prudent *Mahatmas*.

These gurus practiced intense spiritual austerities in their own lives and taught that to others to help them towards emancipation. It is quite evident that mere recitation of these scriptures and *mantras* is not sufficient in itself. Practising that in everyday life is more important. The divine texts or hymns are visible only to the great saints, and therefore their biographies are effective ways of teaching the common man the way to truth and knowledge. Several saints have opined that the sages are the embodiments of the Supreme God.

Love, piety, sanctity do not have shape or form. We know that just like beauty is perceptible only in a mirror, the inner qualities like love, devoutness, sanctity need to be reflected in one's innerself for it to manifest in life properly.

Jesus Christ said, "He hath seen the father who hath seen the son."
Similarly, Mahatma Kabir opined,

"*Alakh purushko aarsee sadhu hi ka dehai,*

Lakh jo chahe alakhko un lekh nahi"

Translation: The body of a saintly person is the mirror to reflect the unseen Lord, One who intends to perceive the unseen should look at the saints.

"Always speak the truth" is a very popular advice and easy to understand, but the suffering this truth engenders for its followers is just as well known!

To ease the suffering of people, the Graceful Almighty sends down the great saints and demi-gods to purify the contaminated state of life and spiritualism. So it is indeed a duty for all of us to study, learn, and discuss the lives of these avatars to see and perceive the truth, the divine light in the soul. It is obvious that the study of such lives compensates for the lack of good, pious company (*satsang*), since finding such pious souls these days is also rare.

To solve this problem, the five ways advised by Mahaprabhu Shri Chaitanya is noteworthy: 1) *Sri Murtira shraddhaya sevana*—worship of the holy deity Shri Krishna; (2) *Nama kirtana*—congregational chanting of the holy Name; (3) *Bhagavata sravana*—regularly listening to holy literature, particularly the Shrimad Bhagavatam; (4) *Mathura vasa*—live in a holy place like a dham; and, (5) *Sadhu sanga*—association with devotees.

Here *Bhagavata sravana* and *Mathura vasa* mean reading/listening to holy books and pilgrimages to holy places repectively. Thus, it is very clear that absorbing the lessons from biographies of the great spiritual saints in one's heart and applying them in life could lead us all to the path of the final destination—God—irrespective of religious affiliations like Shaiva, Shakta, Shaurya, Ganapatya, Vaishnava, Buddhist, Jain, Christian, Muslim.

This humble foreword is only the preface to the biography of the His Holiness Trailanga Swami of the sacred Kashidham—who was an avatar and belonged to the sect of Shri Shri Shankaracharya. The holy Shankaracharya himself belonged to the sect of Gyaan Yogi Bhagavan Sukadeva; and the lineage of these three great sages, in turn, starts from the first guru of the Sanyasi sect (in between the period of Sukadeva and Shankaracharya) called Dattatreya, who was the son of Atri Muni and Anasuya.

Mahatma Sukadeva was the result of the austerities performed by his father Maharshi Krishnadwaipayana Vyasa, who did intense penance in order to get a wise, saintly son. Sukadeva passed sixteen years in his mother's womb so as to prevent getting entrapped with the delusions of material life. His father Vyasadeva came to know about this and took refuge at the lotus-feet of the good Lord Vishnu. Lord Vishnu dispelled the illusions of *maya* just like a mustard seed gets tossed away by the horns of a mad bull.

After that, Sukadeva took birth; this wonderful background reveals the inborn faculties of Sukadeva as a holder of the greatest wisdom right from the outset. Likewise, Shivaguru, the father of Adi Shankaracharya, was the sole child of his father and had no intention to get married, but finally married at the earnest request of his father (who was his grandfather's only son). However, he remained childless for a long time. Towards the latter part of their life, Shivaguru and his wife prayed hard to Lord Shiva and by his grace, Shankara took birth. Shankaracharya and Sukadeva (both of them being great saints) were immaculate, stainless, and unattached to the mundane world. Since birth, they were wonderfully precocious, extremely spiritual and at the same time very humble and devout souls.

Likewise, Trailanga Swami was also the result of his parent's austerity. In early days of his life, he was a disciplined *brahmachari*, a celibate, and intent on becoming an emanicipated soul exonerated from rebirth. He became a tireless and earnest devotee in search of the Supreme but also was deeply absorbed in conventional worship of the physical idols, infusing life to them. From this point of view, Trailanga Swami's life and ideology was more effective than that of Sukadeva and Shankaracharya as the pathfinder to mankind.

Sukadeva was born a saint and never had to go through any austerities. As a prince cannot solve the woes of a suffering poor man without the practical knowledge of paucity of wealth, it was not effective on the part of Sukadeva to meet the spiritual needs of fellow *sadhaks* seeking the ultimate goal.

Shri Shri Sankaracharya, on the other hand, was not a born saint, but a celestially gifted genius and spiritually powerful person who attained proficiency in early childhood. Trailanga Swami also acquired spiritual proficiency in his early days by dint of his superhuman discipline, but his life-long devotional austerities for two hundred and eighty years show us clearly that keen and tireless search for the Supreme can make a soul arrive at the true meaning of life—even without having a lot of inborn divinity.

Trailanga Swami was the living epitome of godliness in human body. Countless wise and elite people as well as the masses considered him the Supreme Lord Shiva of the holy Kashidham.

Swami Adbhutananda (Latu Maharaj) frequently opined that only intense spiritual austerities can bring divinity in a human being—"*Trailanga Swami's was not an easy transformation—it needed long, incessant austerities. Spiritual austerities, intense spiritual austerities, are needed to reach the state of the Supreme Soul incorporated in the human body.*"

Nudity alone does not make one equivalent to a Trailanga Swami. Being unclad does not necessarily bring any pleasure of union with the Divine.

One may not be able to match Trailanga Swami's intense austerities and long search for the Supreme, though all of them who worship the Almighty will get blessings from Him. Thakur Shri Ramakrishna Paramahamsa would say: "*Trailanga Swami sab se paar—his body is like that of a common man—but his deeds are different. He has attained oneness with Lord Shiva. Lord Vishwanath and Trailanga Swami are one and the same.*" (Sat Katha, 2nd part)

Trailanga Swami adviced each and everybody to follow his or her own religion. He did not advocate any epoch-making religious concepts nor establish any new sect, but proved the limitless extension of Sanatana Dharma that is evident throughout his long pious life.

In modern times, amid a selfish and confused humanity, discussion and practice of his advice can bring welfare to us all. All the facts of this great avatar cannot be completely known, especially since he was someone who observed a vow of silence during the last period of his long life.

His Bengali disciple, the late Umacharan Mukhopadhyay, wrote a book on him containing his messages and advice, which was possible only due to the grace of the great sage, who at times narrated stories and incidents from his life to his disciples.

But, unfortunately, not a single copy of that book is currently available at present for it was never printed and published. To bring out the great saint's biography once again, and to meet the need of many readers, we have taken the holy mission to write and publish his life as transparently as possible.

We collected the details and narratives relating his life from Shri Shri Shankari Mataji, his only living disciple who was brought up by Trailanga Swami himself, and who lived her life as an austere celibate and as a devoted saint. This ever-pure, ever-free, pious biography provides bliss to the writer, publisher and, hopefully, to the reader as well.

Due to unavoidable circumstances and the need of the hour, despite our incompetence we have taken this holy mission and are publishing this with our heads bowed down in reverence to the lotus-feet of the holy Lord Trailanga Swamiji.

Chapter 1. Life Long Anchorite—Trailanga Swami

In Vizianagaram, Andhra Pradesh, there was a prosperous village called Holia where a rich Brahmin *zamindar* (land owner) named Narasimha Rao lived over three hundred years ago. His wife Vidyavati Devi was an innately devout and pious soul, accomplished in all aspects. While it is frequently observed that people who become wealthy end up forgetting God and abandon all spiritual pursuits rather quickly, Narasimha Rao and Vidyavati Devi were an exceptional couple in that they never forgot the all-pervading One. Nobody returned from their door without receiving help or generous charity, to the extent that people of Holia would constantly be showering praise on them for their nobility and generosity. This *zamindar* couple chanted holy hymns day in and day out, and lived a peaceful life.

However, they remained childless for a long period; and this was the only unfulfilled desire that they had, which affected their peace at times. Without the sweet voice of an infant filling up their house, their domestic bliss was incomplete.

After a considerable period of being despondent over this, in order to beget children, Narasimha Rao married once again. With unusual tolerance and kindness, Vidyavati Devi welcomed her husband's new wife, in friendship and with affection, and thus peace prevailed in the family.

Vidyavati Devi had been worshiping and praying for a child to Lord Vishwanath for years, and such a pure hearted devotee is never deprived of God's grace.

In December 1607 and in the month of *Poush*, on *Sukla Ekadashi* day, when the moon was in the lunar mansion of the star *Rohini*, Vidyavati Devi gave birth to a male child—at a very auspicious moment according to the almanac. Narasimha Rao became ecstatic and his house was filled with joy and laughter, and he immediately began charitable activities in celebration.

There was a large *Shivalinga* in his family temple that was worshiped regularly by spiritually inclined Vidyavati Devi. One day, a strange yet wonderful incident took place. After the birth of a newborn, when the period where a new mother is supposed to abstain from ritual worship (due to impurity) ended, Vidyavati Devi resumed her worship of Lord Shiva. She kept the baby lying on the *verandah* (porch) of the temple. That day, when she finished her devotional activities and was coming out of the temple, she saw a circle of fire emerging from the body of her newborn son. She became numb with shock and fright, but to her surprise, she saw that the baby was unhurt and moreover his body was shining with a strange light that appeared divine. She became very afraid after this strange incident. However, later when her husband heard about this incident and opined that the significance of this event meant the baby was a boon from Lord Shiva, her joy was unbounded. Narasimha Rao assured his wife not to be anxious.

Shri Shri Mataji heard the narration of this incident directly from her guru Trailanga Swami.

Vidyavati Devi brought up her blessed son with motherly love and devout attention. The baby was named 'Shivaram' Trailanga Swami. He was named Telang Swami initially due to his origins in the erstwhile Telangana state.

Later on, since he had risen above gender identification—he was also called 'Trailinga', as one beyond the sexual states of human beings.

Some days later, the second wife of Narasimha Rao also became the proud mother of a male child who was named Shridhar by his parents. Both were calm and quiet by nature, and with sharp intellects. Shivaram displayed his divine faculties early, by learning and acquiring knowledge quite easily. He learnt many *shastras* (scriptures) at an early age. The other remarkable aspect about him was his complete disinterest in sports and typical boyhood activities and mischief.

He was very quiet by nature and had this deep sense of gravitas on his face all the time. He loved to watch other boys playing in the fields, busy at their favourite games, but he himself never played with them. Quite frequently, he could be seen lost in some divine, trance-like state.

We often notice in the biographies of great spiritual figures like Trailanga Swami that they all were seemingly inspired by some unknown fountainhead of spiritualism, which helped their attempts to re-establish religious sanctity and increase devotion among people.

Whenever he was in the contemplative state, he looked exceedingly handsome, as if encircled by a divine light. His physical stature was that of a well-built person—wide forehead, splendourous, wide eyes, sharp nose, a wide chest, soft skin with hands reaching below the knees (*ajanubahu*), and several other physical characteristics that are the hallmarks of great spiritual souls. He seemed perpetually to be in a state of bliss, or *ananda*.

As youth approached, the young Shivaram became increasingly grave, without showing any signs of being affected by sensual desires, as is normal for boys of his age. The young man appeared to be constantly merged in the boundless deep of the Divine. He had overcome lust by spiritual practices, and had begun meditating with intense devotion towards attaining self-realisation. His nature had the placidity of a calm ocean, showing complete indifference to the ups and downs of life and the hustle and bustle of society.

Everyone who saw him could not help but be astonished at the sight of the aura of unstained peace that he exuded. Narasimha Rao, though, had become anxious realising his son's detachment from all things mundane, and could not fathom the depth of his spirituality. He started making arrangements to lead young Shivaram towards matrimony and a householder's life; but Shivaram's innate instincts prevented any such thought from arising in his mind, and he was thus protected. He expressed his sentiments to his father that the common life held no attraction for him since it was not permanent, and his only desire was to reach the altar of God.

Vidyavati, his mother, considered her son's desire with reverence and opined that if he indeed reaches his goal, it would bring great blessings and honor to their family. In the meanwhile, Shridhar, being the other son, would be the one who could keep the dynasty alive. In retrospect, only a mother as blessed and spiritual as she could have borne such a great son! Narasimha Rao agreed with his wife, and Shivram was touched by his mother's words and wishes; and was highly inspired to the very depths of his heart. .

He received *upadesha* from his mother, and began intense austerities.

People usually become spiritually inclined and detached from normal life only when unbearable tragedies happen to them and when they realise the impermance of life, but it is rare indeed to see someone willfully choosing the spiritual path. Shivaram could have also led a life of luxury and run after temporary riches and impermanent pleasures, but he was divinely ordained to lead his blessed life in search of the Ultimate Truth.

॥ ॐ तत् सत् ॥

|| om tat sat ||

Chapter 2. Demise of Parents

Shivaram's first and foremost Guru was Vidyavati Devi, who initiated her spiritually inclined son with a *mantra* (*mantra deeksha*).He received the instructions with deep devotion, and was happy living an austere life wholly devoted to spiritual pursuits.

Life is a great examiner—like a goldsmith who melts gold in order to purify it, God ignites us with the fire of woes and worries, and thus purifies our souls. He examines our innermost self with the touchstone of suffering, sorrow, and pain, and sometimes he tests our humane qualities by giving a happy life of fun and pleasure. Only the one who can accept struggles and comforts with the same humility and remain calm in his heart can receive the grace of God. One who does not resort to dishonesty or unethical ways in order to avoid the ups and downs and thorny roads of life is indeed blessed. It is indeed a struggle to triumph over the tests set by God by bowing down to His will. With aimless and countless desires, one can never know the Supreme Reality. It is akin to one floating like a rudderless ship in the ocean and thereby never reaching the harbor. These kinds of tests were due for Shivaram too, as one day his life became clouded as well. His father Narasimha Rao became severely ill, and passed away after five days of agony. From that moment on, his devoted wife Vidyavati gave up family life, and devoted herself exclusively to worship of the divine. Shivaram also followed his mother in this path.

After twelve years of austere life as a widow, Vidyavati Devi also breathed her last, not only making Shivaram an orphan, but also leaving a vacuum in the life of the people of Holia. The normal peace and calm that was always visible within Shivaram also got affected—but the blazing pyre of his departed mother dispelled the last of the doubts from his heart, and he became absolutely free from any interest in mundane matters thereafter.

Smearing himself with the holy ashes from his mother's funeral pyre, he began intense spiritual austerities there. His soul was completely purified in the process. Usually, such a tragedy can shatter one's mental resolve, but Shivaram was strong enough to accept such a loss with remarkable fortitude. The pain of his mother's loss transformed into the nectar of divine grace for him.

Thus, the last of the shackles tying Shivaram to his mundane life at the age of 52 were broken. However, the younger brother Shridhar became disturbed on seeing the renunciation of his elder brother. Though Shridhar himself could have become the sole heir to the vast riches left by his father and thus materially very happy, he possessed a noble, loving heart, and so was fervently longing and trying for his elder brother's return to the family life, but in vain.

In this manner, he became like a Bharata of the *Kali Yuga* (the age of vice)—of impeccable character, he was not happy with the material riches left by his elder brother at the cost of his elder brother's total departure from their family.

One who tastes the real nectar that is the essence of the Divine, that soul will never care for anything else! He alone holds the key to the supreme treasure—the grace of the Almighty—and is thus lost in the *dhyaan* (contemplation) of the Absolute.

Shivaram paid no heed to anybody's request to go back to his family life. With sweet words, he made them understand that for the soul that has the grace of God, nothing mundane is attractive anymore.

He said to his younger brother gently and affectionately, "*Brother! I have taken this path of renunciation with the blessings and permission of our parents when they both were alive. You are well aware of it. They are no more with us, and I would like you to enjoy the material wealth that they left behind, but please do not call me back to this worldly existence. I am helpless. I cannot take myself back from the feet of the King of all kings. I request you to not try to draw me anymore in the matters mundane. God bless you!*"

Shridhar returned home sad and despondent. But his magnanimous heart was not ready to draw the line of separation between his beloved elder brother and himself. He did not even think that all the responsibilities and duties on his part towards his elder brother had ended. To alleviate any physical discomforts his elder brother would face as a hermit dwelling under the bare sky, he established a 'Bhajan Ashram' there in the cremation grounds, and also arranged for regular food and other amenities.

Shivaram lived there and continued his search for the Supreme, with the vast, yet secluded, open environment as his only companion allowing him to meditate in peace. In the ceaselessly expanded grey beauty there, Shivaram saw the holy Lord Shiva's silver mountain like home, he heard the hymns in the chirping of birds, felt the snowwhite touch of the good Lord. In this manner, the great devotee passed twenty years of his ascetic life.

Gradually he began to feel an irresistible urge to embark on a holy pilgrimage. He became eager to be in the company of holy saints, and receive the initiatory prayers (*deeksha*) from an ideal guru. For every spiritual aspirant following the tradition of *Sanatana Dharma* (Hinduism), it is recommended to practice spiritual austerities under the guidance of a suitable guru. No one can make sufficient spiritual progress without receiving *deeksha* on their own. Even the greatest of devotees like Dhruva had to take *deeksha* from Maharshi Narada. Shivaram had become worthy enough after years of self-restraint, patience, and tolerance. Soon, God Himself made his *deeksha* possible as no honest devotion goes in vain. After all, the Supreme Lord is called as '*Vancha Kalpataru*'—the tree that fulfills all desires.

Very soon the day came, when a famous old Swami– Swami Bhagirathanandaji—reached Shivaram's hut at the cremation ground. The Swami originally hailed from the village Bastur in Patiala, Punjab. They lived in proximity for days and eventually got attracted to each other. This indeed was pre-ordained by God—it was just waiting for the right time to come to fruition. Finally, Shivaram left Holia and roamed for six years, finally reaching the holy pilgrimage center Pushkar.

In 1685, at the age of 78, Shivaram received the *mantra deeksha* (initiation) from Swami Bhagirathanandaji, and began to learn yoga. At that time, he was named after Swami Ganapati Saraswati. But as he was born in the Telugu-speaking state Telangana, he became more famous over time as Telang Swami. Also since he had gone beyond gender idenfitication, he was also called Trailanga Swami. The *shastras* (scriptures) opine that '*guruseva*' (service to the guru) is one of the most important parts of *sadhana*. Shri Shri Bhagwan Lord Krishna said in the holy Bhagavad Gita that *Gyan Sadhana*—devotion for wisdom requires devotion to the guru.

तद्विद्धि प्रणिपातेन परिप्रश्नेन सेवया।

उपदेक्ष्यन्तै ते ज्ञानं ञानिनस्तत्वदर्शिनः ॥

tadviddhi praṇipātena paripraśnena sevayā |
upadekṣyantai te jñānaṁ ñāninastatvadarśinaḥ ||

(The Bhagavad Gita – 4:34)

Translation: *This knowledge should be learned by accepting a spiritual master and by submissive inquiries and rendering service unto him. The self-realised and holy saint endowed with divine revelation will instruct you in wisdom.*

According to the Shrimad Bhagavatam:

आचार्यं मां विज्ञानीयात्

ācāryaṁ māṁ vijñānīyāt

(Shrimad Bhagavatam – 11:17:27)

Translation: *Know God and your guru as inseparable—merged in oneself.*

In the opinion of the Vedanta also, the devotion to acquire knowledge (*Gyan Sadhana*) needs two steps to follow: 1) *Tatwatta vichar*—ascertainment of the Divine Truth and 2) devotional service to the guru. Devoted dedication in the caring service of the guru consecrates the soul of a disciple and he becomes worthy of meeting a true guru.

Shivaram, who was the ideal disciple, stayed in close proximity to his Guru and continued his spiritual austerities. In this manner, ten years passed by when in the year 1695 Swami Bhagirathanandji breathed his last at Pushkar. After that event, Trailanga Swami also left the place at the age of eighty eight as an unclad (*digambara*) mendicant.

Traveling across many places, he reached Setubandha Rameswaram situated in the southern tip of India. Then he traveled further north and lived for three years in the holy Dwarka Dham and Sudamapuri, and afterwards went to Nepal when he was over 90 years old. There he stayed in a completely absorbed state of *samadhi* for six years, after which he visited pilgrimage places like Kedarnath, Badrinath, Gangotri, and Yamunotri in the Uttarakhand state.

Then he left on a sojourn of 19 years into Tibet at Manasarovar. Thus he passed long 25 years in the lap of the Himalayas, after which he then went to the banks of the river Narmada and reached the Markandeya Ashram. There he came across a great saint Khakee Baba. After 6 years, he went to the holy Triveni in Prayag and spent 4 more years there doing *sadhana*. Finally, he went to the holy city of Varanasi in 1737 at the age of 130 years. Except for a short tour once, Trailanga Swami stayed at Varanasi for a long period of 150 years.

The great saint Shri Bhagwan Gangopadhyay used to live in Varanasi with his two great disciples—Loknath Brahamachari and Benimadhav Gangopadhyay—for years. Before taking *samadhi*, he entrusted his disciples to the tutelage of Trailanga Swami. After completion of their education, Loknath and Benimadhav set out for various holy places and later returned to Varanasi.

Then Trailanga Swami, their guru, set out for a separate tour with the intention of traveling up to the polar region with his disciples, i.e., Loknath Brahmachari, Benimadhav Gangopadhyay, and another disciple, the holy Muslim sage fakir Abdul Gafoor.

As Loknath and Benimadhav and the others became unable to travel up to the polar region, Trailanga Swami advised them to return and himself continued the journey. Finally he reached the polar region and saw Udayachal at the easternmost surface of Mother Earth. He returned to Varanasi after some years.

In this way, Trailanga Swami completed his circumnavigation crossing mountains, rivers, forests, countries, pilgrimage cities of many countries and finally started living in Varanasi. He was worshiped by countless devotees who considered him as the personification of Lord Shiva Himself. Countless fortunate men were bestowed with his blessings, and innumerable men could select the right path of spiritual disciple by his holy grace for a long long span of time.

॥ ॐ तत् सत् ॥

|| om tat sat ||

Chapter 3. Trailanga Swami and His Yoga Vibhuti

From the perspective of great sages, excessive popularity is not desirable, but complete avoidance of society is also a bar as it goes against their message and necessity of mass welfare. A swarm of bees will come and take honey from a flower in full bloom, but they also bring with them—and leave behind— dirt from their legs on the petals. Similarly, the magnanimity and uncommon divinity of great sages are rarely hidden from the masses, so they will be attracted to divine souls with ulterior motives for fulfillment of material desires.

Some come bearing expensive gifts as a form of a bribe, a few others will try to offer and feed them rich food, some come hoping for grace and thus most come hoping to fulfill their material and sensory desires. Some want children; others want to be rich and materially wealthy. All such matters mundane disturb the spiritual practices of these great souls. In Trailanga Swami's case as well, often his superhuman abilities or *siddhis* were quite apparent to the masses and this, is turn, attracted people who annoyed him no end.

Compelled by the unwanted assembly of crowds, Trailanga Swami had to often leave his place in search of peace and solitude. But just as it is hard to hide a fire, it was difficult for his presence to remain hidden for long.

Whenever he saw any soul suffering, out of deep compassion he used his abilities to provide it with divine grace and mercy, leading to people thronging near him and hampering his efforts at *sadhana*, as a result of which he could not stay at one place for long. Such incidents occurred frequently in his lifetime, and it merits a closer look.

As a result of his intense *sadhana* and austerities, Trailanga Swami had obtained *siddhis* like *Anima* (reducing the physical body to an infinitesimally small size), *Laghima* (becoming weightless), *Mahima* (expanding one's body to an infinitely large size), *Garima* (becoming infinitely heavy), *Prapti* (having unrestricted access to all places), *Prakamya* (realising whatever one desires), *Vashitva* (control over all including the five elements), and *Ishitva* (command over the activities of the entire earthly being and matters/omnipotence).

These powers are called the *Ashtasiddhis. H*owever, these are not the primary mission of any real spiritual aspirant. To reach the altar of God is the only mission to accomplish, and along this path the acquisition of *Ashtasiddhi* happens by divine grace. But it is also evident that often, the way of accomplishment on the part of spiritual aspirants is not always free of temptation—some times they deviate from the right path. Quite frequently these aspirants become proud having acquired a few of the *siddhis* and thus ruin themselves.

Kenopanishad narrates a story that when the *devas* (deities) got filled with pride over their victory over the *asuras* (demons) and became ecstatic, the Supreme Shakti Adya Devi outshined their pride and practically made them aware that but for Her, the Lord of Fire Agni cannot burn even a tiny blade of grass, and the Lord of Wind/Air Pavan is unable to blow out even the finest blades of grass!!

Ashtasiddhi could never tempt the pious heart of Trailanga Swami; on the contrary, he was indifferent to the powers he had gained. He perceived God's grace even in the spiritual wealth he was bestowed with and so he was never proud.

When some one acquires divine power or *siddhis* of such kind because of intense spiritual austerities and then becomes proud over possessing such abilities, then all such blessings that he received inevitably become useless and become causes of their downfall. Such sadhus resume their unfinished spiritual pursuits once again after their transmigration on the earth; and usually these are the persons who are born in rich families or an abode of a yogi. But Trailanga Swamiji did not let these *siddhis* distract or tempt him from accomplishing the Divine or pursuit of the Supreme Reality, and for this he was adored as the *Saghai Vishwanath* of the holy Kashidham.

Now, questions may be asked as to what then, was the aim of giving such demonstrations of his superhuman powers? If, demonstration of such powers were not his intention, then why did he do so in public?

Such things happen spontaneously without any effort by the great sages. This comes as naturally to them as the emergence of the sun from the depth of the dark night. Though these great souls are vast mines of many such riches, it is actually their divinity—the power of the Almighty God—that actually shines out through them, who otherwise live by the same rules of human existence. They do not have to put any effort into such exhibition of their divine powers.

Like pieces of dry wood that quickly reduce to ashes whenever set alight by fire, the people who have become free from selfish desires likewise receive the benevolent grace of these saints. They become recipients of blessings and boons. The *sat-chit-ananda* (existence-knowledge-bliss) state that Trailanga Swami was perpetually in is obviously beyond our comprehension.

It was impossible on his part to lust for fame and fortune by exhibiting his divine powers. Nature did its own work, while the Swamiji stayed behind the curtain, considering himself a non-factor of any such exhibition of his inner strength. The incomprehensible magnanimity of God was manifested through the great Swami—he was only the medium.One may note that miracles and unusual incidents have always been evident in lives of such great saints.

On the other hand, with our limited perception, we sometimes see the ordinary as something supernatural. We are unable to distinguish between heaven and earth. It is not hard to believe that divinity can descend to the meagre plane of common life. Yogis and saints are the only true mirrors through which we can watch the reflection of the Almighty's power. The common man is a slave to the six vices (*Shad Ripu*) i.e.lust (*kama*), greed (*lobha*), anger (*krodha*), pride (*mada*), attachment (*moha*), and covetousness (*matsarya*), and this conditioning leads to a weakness in comprehension due to which they consider anything beyond their experience as being supernatural and extraordinary.

Indeed, there are only a few who try to condition their mind and soul and improve the purity of their inner selves by meditation and *sadhana* tirelessly. However, these activities that are natural to these spiritual aspirants are perceived as unnatural by the majority of the common people who cannot understand their purpose. By using such *siddhis* gained after tremendous austerities, the great sages have demonstrated to people since ages that love for God and love for God's subjects and creation are co-related—one cannot exist without the other.

This is a common aspect of all the great saints that we see or hear about; it is not possible for them to love God without loving God's creations. They perceive the majesty of God in each and every part of creation, and become enthralled by it. Just like an average person who is in love will pay great attention and care to his lover and the relationship, likewise, great sages who deeply love God cannot remain indifferent to the creation of their beloved Master. So, whenever, wherever true saints see suffering in any of the God's creations, they try to do everything they can in their power to provide respite, but such all-merciful saints are really rare in the world.

Once the great saint Shri Ramakrishna Paramahamsa met a person called Mani Mullick who had come to meet him after having traveled (traveled) to Varanasi. Shri Ramakrishna inquired if Mani Mullick had met any holy people there. On hearing that Mani had the chance to meet Trailanga Swami, Shri Ramakrishna asked what Mani Mullick thought of him. Mani Mullick replied, "*People say Trailanga Swami has lost his spiritual powers and these days he performs fewer miracles than before*."

Shri Ramakrishna got annoyed on hearing these words and brushed it off by saying, "*These are statements made by ignorant people trying to find fault with the Swami*." Ignorant men could not fathom the true depth of the truly God-realised souls like Trailanga Swami, but Shri Ramakrishna Paramahamsa, the great avatara of the last century, paid no heed to such statements.

॥ ॐ तत् सत् ॥

|| om tat sat ||

Chapter 4. Some examples of Yogavibhuti

In the Bengali Calendar year 1104 (1697 CE), Trailanga Swami stayed for some time in Rameswaram. An annual festival celebrated in that area was a fair during the month of *Karthika*. Many people from all walks of life would assemble there. A considerable number of sadhus and spiritual aspirants too would attend

Once, a certain Brahmin died during his stay at the fair. A crowd had gathered encircling his dead body. Trailanga Swami saw the dead man's companions lamenting loudly and making arrangements for his funeral. Trailanga Swamiji felt their pain and empathised, and suddenly took some water from his *kamandalu* (water pot) and sprinkled it on the corpse. A few minutes later, everybody became flabbergasted on seeing the dead body slowly come to life. In the meanwhile, Swamiji quickly left the place, but some villagers from his native village Holia, who were present there, recognised him and began to request him to return to his own land. Swamiji gently dissuaded them with sweet words. But the news of the Brahmin's revival spread like wildfire in no time.

To avoid the crowds disturbing him, Swamiji left Rameswaram and went to the remote town of Sudamapuri near Dwarkadham. A man from Sudamapuri had seen the Swamiji at Rameswaram, and so he immediately became attracted to the Swami. He began to take sincere care of the Swami with true devotion. Satisfied by his good pious nature and careful service towards his comfort, Swamiji blessed him; and soon not only did the fortunate man acquire plenty of wealth, but even a son was born in his childless home. Once again, word spread out and people began to assemble and encircle him disturbing his spiritual practices and austerities.

Next, the Swamiji took refuge in a dense peaceful forest in Nepal. But even in this place infested by snakes and wild animals, his presence got noticed.

One day, the chief of the army to the King of Nepal went into the forest on a hunting expedition. He aimed at a tiger and missed. The frightened tiger rushed to the depths of the forest chased by the hunter who was on a speeding horse. Then the hunter saw an amazing scene and became completely immobilised. He dared not move anymore after seeing that the tiger had taken refuge at the feet of a large bodied sadhu, one seemingly having a divine form as if he were Lord Shiva Himself. The sadhu's divine contemplation got interrupted at hearing the roars coming from the tiger. He gently reassured the tiger by patting him affectionately and the animal responded to the pats like a pet cat. The chief of army staff from Nepal watched this unfold and stood there stupefied. He was completely bewildered and was wondering if it was indeed the Lord Mahadeva Himself before his eyes.

The sadhu was none other than the great Trailanga Swami. Swamiji understood his confusion and called him calmly. The chief stood near him with awe and bowed down before him. Swamiji smiled and told him, "*My son, don't get scared. Just look at the tiger's calm demeanor. You have just been trying to kill it; however this animal can kill you right now. Just try to understand nobody can kill anybody. The tiger has become non-violent and so have you. Shed off the lust of violence from your mind for good and see no one as your enemy. Remember that love begets love. Be brave and go back now.*" The chief knelt before the divine-looking sage and went back. Later the tiger also fled from there. When the King of Nepal came to hear about this incident from his army chief, he was amazed. Then the pious king went to meet Trailanga Swami, accompanied by his men carrying valuable presents and knelt down before the great saint with sincere devotion. Swamiji, too, accepted him cordially and blessed him, giving him invaluable spiritual advice. However, he didnt accept anything from the heap of presents. The monarch also realised that a saint has no material wants, and did not feel disappointed about this. He touched Swamiji's holy feet once again and returned to Kathmandu.

The news of the incident spread fast in Nepal. The forests got crowded and no longer provided solitude, so Swamiji had to leave the place. He crossed the Himalayan ranges on foot and reached Tibet in the year 1707. He was in sojourn in that area for three years and then in 1710 he went to the shores of Manasarovar.

A widow who lived at Manasarovar had just lost her seven-year-old son due to snake bite. The lamenting lady took her son to the cremation ground with tears in her eyes, quite like Shaivya, the wife of Raja Harishchandra, who took their dead son Rohitashwa's body to the cremation ground while crying. Her companions were beginning to arrange for the dead body's cremation, when it appeared as if the cries of despair had caught the attention of the merciful God and Trailanga Swami came there. The distraught mother regained her hopes when she saw the Swami and exclaimed, "*Lord Shiva Himself has come to save my son's life.*" She began to weep at the Swami's feet. Then the all-merciful Swamiji touched the dead body of the young boy and yet another miracle occurred when the boy slowly started showing signs of life. The widowed mother immediately took her son into her lap, but when her eyes looked around for the mysterious saviour, he could not be seen. From that point on, no one saw Trailanga Swami at Manasarovar.

It was at the Markandeya Ashram on the bank of the river Narmada, where Swamiji re-appeared in the year 1133 (1726 CE). He lived there with some other pious sadhus where he would spend his nights completely absorbed in meditation.

Khakee Baba was another saint who lived there at that time. One day he saw an astonishing sight unfolding in front of him on the banks of the Narmada. To his amazement, he saw that the river seemed to be flowing with milk instead of water and Trailanga Swamij was drinking the milk with his cupped hands. The amazed Khakee Baba also wanted to drink milk from the river, but the moment he touched the flowing river, it no longer appeared to be milk but was plain old river water. In the meanwhile Trailanga Swami had gone back and resumed his yogic posture for meditation. Khakee Baba was speechless for quite a while after having seen such an astonishing sight. He rushed back to the ashram and described the amazing incident in detail to the fellow ashramities. Thereafter the Swamiji was viewed by the others as an exalted saint with powerful *siddhis* and so they began to worship him. Swamiji decided to leave and in the year 1140 (1733 CE) after a seven-year stay, he left Markandeya Ashram and went to the holy Prayag *Tirtha* (Allahabad) and after locating a tranquil place that gave him solitude, he resumed *sadhana*.

Once, Swamiji was absorbed in the contemplation of the Divine near the confluence of three rivers Ganga, Yamuna, and Saraswati near the Triveni Prayag Tirtha Ghat. It was raining heavily, and so the typical assembly of people at the *ghat* started dispersing, but Trailanga Swami remained unmoved. A Bengali Brahmin, Ramtaran Bhattacharjee who knew Swamiji very well, was present there, and he immediately got busy trying to prevent the Swamiji from getting drenched. He repeatedly requested Swamiji to leave the place for a nearby shelter. Swamiji told Ramratan, "*Please don't worry for my sake. I am perfectly at home here, and moreover I cannot leave this place right now, as I know a boat coming near this ghat carrying quite a few people will capsize very soon. I have to rescue the boarders.*"

Right then in front of the Brahmin's eyes, an approaching boat began to capsize due to the heavy winds. At the same time, the Swami was also no longer visible anywhere. After a short while, a confused Ramtaram saw that the boat with its boarders was floating completely fine and without any apparent damage, and finally it reached the shore. When the boarders saw the unclad sadhu coming down from the boat, they could not understand as to what had happened, but they fell at his feet in gratitude and went away. Ramtaran was also standing there with wonder-struck eyes. Coming back to senses, he prostrated on the ground to salute the Swamiji with deep reverence in his heart. Swamiji said, "*My son, be easy, it is nothing remarkable to be amazed about. The Almighty God is present everywhere with infinite strength and grace. We too are empowered by that same infinite power, but our addiction to sensory pleasures and material greed negates our entire strength and turns us into slaves of meanness. We never care about spiritual upliftment, or try to achieve purity of heart. Otherwise man is also immensely powerful as God Himself is the source of power of his creations. The man who knows this truth and honors this power within can do anything easily without fail. Don't get soaked any more. Go back to your own place.*"

Ramtaran could not see him any more after that incident, as Trailanga Swami had already gone away from that place. Later, he was seen in the holy Kashidham.

|| ॐ तत् सत् ||

|| om tat sat ||

Chapter 5. Sachal Vishwanath of Kashidham

During his stay in the garden of Tuslidas near the Asi Ghat, Trailanga Swami used to go to the Lolark Kund (pond) quite often. One day, he accidentaly touched a leper from Ajmer named Brahma Singh with his holy feet while he was sleeping. Awakened by his touch of mercy, the leper began to worship the Swamiji with folded hands, treating the gigantic sage standing before his eyes as a manifestation of Lord Shiva Himself. Brahma Singh had already suffered quite a bit for his past karmas.The omniscient Swami gave him a bilva leaf from the Bael tree (*Aegle Marmelos*) and said, "*My son, you will get respite from this malady if you take a dip in the water of the kund with sincere belief and respectful heart, it is beyond any doubt.*" His blessings had the miraculous power to treat an otherwise incurable condition. Brahma Singh became free of his afflicted physical condition, and was back to being his handsome, normal self. Thereafter, he became one of Trailanga Swami's countless lifelong devotees.

After this incident, to avoid inquisitive crowds, Swamiji set out for the ashram of Maharshi Veda Vyasa in Haridwar. One day, on the banks of the river Ganga, as usual, a crowd of people had gathered intending to bathe in the the sacred water. A person afflicted with tuberculosis was also in the crowd, also with the same intent of taking a bath in the Ganges.

Despondent after suffering with this disease for a long time, he had come to the holy Kashidham to spend the rest of his shortened life. Suddenly he started choking and became unconscious. A few people in the crowd tried hard to provide relief in whatever way they could, but it seemed nothing could change the patient's fate. All of a sudden, Trailanga Swami appeared before the ailing man and began to pass his soothing hand slowly over his chest. The patient slowly began to regain consciousness. When he saw the large-statured saint in front of him, he felt a deep awe within as if he was in front of Lord Shiva Himself.

Falling at the feet of the great saint, he began to fervently pray for relief from his disease with tears in his eyes. Swamiji took pity on him. He took a lump of Ganges mud in his palm and after sanctifying it, he gave the man the lump of mud and adviced him to swallow it after performing his ablutions in the holy Ganges. Then he himself took a dip in the Ganges water. When the man followed the instructions given by Trailanga Swami, he was immediately freed from the disease. The man was a Bengali Brahmin called Sitanath Bandyopadhyay. And for the rest of his life, Sitanath worshiped Swamiji with sincere devotion as if he was worshiping the manifestation of Lord Shiva Himself.

Once, a man died of snake-bite near Asi Ghat in Kashi. According to the traditions of the time, dead bodies of people who died due to snake bites were not cremated; instead they were tied to rafts made of banana stalks and set afloat on the river. The kith and kin of the young man were making arrangements for this, when Swamiji happened to come there and got moved by compassion for the young widow of the dead man.

Quietly, he smeared the scar-mark of snake bite on the dead body with a little Ganges-mud, and then dived into the Ganges and disappeared. No one in the funeral party knew who he was. After a short while, the dead body started showing signs of life, much to the bewilderment and sheer astonishment of everyone assembled. The man finally became conscious, and became uneasy as he was still tied up to the raft. His companions looked at him with wide eyes in shock, and then began to inquire about the reasons as to how the dead person became alive again. Finally, they found out that it was the divine power of Trailanga Swami that made the impossible happen.

Swamiji moved from that place once again, and next began to stay at the Hanuman Ghat. A Marathi woman would take a path adjacent to the mentioned *ghat*, as she was a regular worshiper of Lord Shiva. One day while on that path she suddenly came across the Swami who was completely naked and felt terribly ashamed and embarrassed. While it did not affect the Swami in the least since social etiquette did not really apply to him, it did affect the lady, and she cursed him and called him all kinds of bad names and then went away. But on that night she had a wonderful dream. In her dream, she saw Lord Shiva with the *trishul* (Trident) in his hands telling her, "*Your desires will remain unfulfilled: without the mercy of the naked sadhu whom you had abused today for his nakedness your prayers will have no effect.*" She woke up perspiring profusely after having seen a dream like this. She started trembling with fright and was filled with contrition. She was repentant and at last decided to go to the sadhu to apologise and seek his mercy. She went to Swamiji at the earliest hour of the next morning and washed his holy feet with her tears of repentance. Swamiji was *Ashutosh* (one who is easily satisfied) like Lord Shiva and graciously forgave her. He came to know from the woman that she had been worshiping Lord Shiva for the remedy of a scar in her husband's stomach. The kind hearted living manifestation of Lord Shiva gave her a pinch of ashes, and due to the effect of those holy ashes her husband became free from his ailment. Once again, after news of this incident spread, in order to avoid the crowds Swamiji had to again leave the place. He next went to the famous Dashaswamedh Ghat and stayed there for some years.

In 1788 a king came to visit the holy city of Kashi with his family, and one day went to the Dashaswamedh Ghat on foot to take holy dips in the river water. The route from his temporary dwelling to the *ghat* was covered with canopies for his queen, who used to stay behind the curtains. His sentries prevented any commoners from venturing along that canopied road, as it was specially set up for the privacy and dignity of the royal couple. However, when the queen was getting out of the water after taking a bath in the holy Ganges, she saw the naked *sanyasi* in front of her in broad day light. She got terribly ashamed and fled with her companions immediately, almost running. The king became furious and got the naked saint arrested and brought over to his place.

On asking as to how the *sanyasi* had reached the ghat without the sentries stopping him, he got no answers. People present there requested the king to let the sadhu go, as he was a *sanyasi* for whom social norms did not apply. The king got convinced by their arguments and set the saint free. However, some of the king's men hurled insults and verbally abused the sadhu quite a bit. The saint did not pay any attention to their words and went away, but things did not end there. The king saw in his dream a large figure with white skin and a mass of matted hair, clad in tiger skin and holding a *trishul* roaring at him in furious voice, "*You sinner! You understood who Trailanga Swami was, yet you allowed your men to defame and abuse him in your presence and thus it is you who have dishonored me. You do not deserve to stay in this holy place, get lost from here without delay otherwise you are ruined.*" The king woke up startled by the nightmare, after which he cried out in fear and lost his consciousness.

Once one of Trailanga Swami's disciples, who was a Brahmin pundit named Shri Kedarnath Vachaspati, took Swamiji to his residence wishing to feed him. When the food was being eaten, Swamiji requested

Vachaspati to give him some water to drink. Vachaspati went away to fetch some water, and on his return, was surprised to see the Swamiji drinking water to heart's content. There was no one there who could've given water to the Swamiji. Vachaspati was embarrassed, but learnt the lesson that a thirsty guest must be attended to carefully.

One day, the King of Ujjain was coming to Manikarnika Ghat from the royal palace of the King of Kashi. He became speechless on seeing a man sitting on the surface of the river. On making inquiries, he found out that the person with such amazing abilities was a great yogi called Trailanga Swami. He was told that the Swami had unfettered access to all water, land, and ethereal areas. On hearing about all these abilities of the sage, the king wished to take him on his boat and the omniscient sage himself took the initiative to fulfill the king's wishes. The Maharaja was dumbstruck when he personally experienced Trailanga Swami's spiritual powers and saw that he could probe deep into anyone and that nothing was hidden from him.

The king had a nice sword in his hand, gifted by the British government to honor his courage. The childlike sage wished to have a closer look at the sword, and the king gladly handed it over to him. The great sage had a close look at the sword, and then suddenly threw it into the Ganges instead of handing it back to its owner.

The Maharaja lost his patience and did not hide his anger at this act. When Swamiji was about to leave the boat and land on the bank, the king prevented him from doing so. He intended to punish the sage and thus satisfy his desire for revenge. Swamiji smiled sweetly at him, and immediately put his hands in the river water and drew out two identical swords. He then asked the king to identify his own sword from the two. But the king could not do so, and lowered his head in shame. In a voice as deep as the rumbling of the clouds, Trailanga Swami told the king, "*My son, you are unable to identify your own possessions. I see you as a man who likes to flaunt his wealth, and full of ignorance. You cannot take this sword with you to the after world. How can it be your own which you cannot take with you during your final journey? Why are you feeling angry for anything that does not belong to you?"* Then the Swami handed over one of the two swords to the king and threw the other one into the river. The king realised the greatness of the sage and pleaded for forgiveness for his behaviour and his infatuation with material posessions. Swamiji forgave him and then disappeared into the Ganges.

Once, a celebrated lawyer of the Calcutta High Court came to visit the holy city of Kashi. He had the habit of ridiculing idolatry, as in his mind he felt that idol-worshiping was nothing more than a play with puppets.He would visit the temples of Viswanath, Annapurna with a mocking attitude, but paid no respects or showed obeisance anywhere, since for him worshiping idols was a far cry.

According to Hindu scriptures, after the *darshan* (seeing) of deities, kings, and saints, it is considered auspicious to offer things in worship. Those who are poor can offer flowers, leaves, fruits—even the betel nut or the Indian gooseberries (the yellow myrobalan) are acceptable—as per their ability. Unfortunately, many people are completely ignorant of this.

The lawyer came to hear about the wonderful stories about Swamiji, including that he was at least 300 years old by then. The lawyer was keen on having some fun at the Swami's expense, and with such none-too-noble intentions he went to the Swamiji's place.

He stood at a corner among the throngs who had gathered there and watched him silently. When suddenly someone caught him by the neck and threw him on to the feet of the sage. He suddenly heard some gruff voice saying to him, "*You arrogant fellow! You are so proud of your little knowledge of English that you have forsaken all the religious activities and rituals of Hinduism! For your own good, seek forgiveness from this august personage.*"

The lawyer could not understand what was happening, but when he touched the holy feet of the great sage Trailanga Swami, he felt an intense pleasure and felt as if his heart were dancing. He immediately realised the greatness of his religion and became pure of heart by the merciful touch of the holy sage. He regained his lost faith in Hinduism and its rituals, and thereafter lived a life of a normal pious devotee.

On another occasion, Swamiji indicated that two Bengali Babus should leave the place when they were about to touch his feet. One of them was ready to do so, but the other was not. Swamiji called the attendant who was responsible for the cows within the ashram to take him out but even then the man was not ready to leave the place.

Then the attendant said, "*Babu, you have seen Swamiji, now please leave, since he does not like any crowds here gathering around him.*"

In response, the man angrily and defiantly pushed the attendant and said, "*You may leave if you want, but I won't go.*" The attendant was about react to this when the Swami interjected and asked the man to be quiet and instructed his disciple Brahmachari Mangal Bhatt to bring a piece of paper and a pen.

There was a wall adjacent to the altar, the seat of the Swami, with *shlokas* (holy verses) inscriptions made in Devanagari script. Swamiji began to point to letters from the inscribed *shlokas* in sequence, and Mangal Bhatt began to write them accordingly.

When the process was completed, the complete text was read out for the Babu—"*Babu, you have left your pair of shoes purchased at the cost of eighteen rupees outside the room and came in to see me. Your mind is anxious about those shoes and worried about somebody stealing them. You do not have a right to be here with me in that state of mind; please leave with your shoes.*"

On hearing this, the Babu confessed that he was indeed really anxious about his shoes and then he calmed down. He quietly left the place without any further argument.

A man named Shri Joy Gopal Karmakar, who was originally a resident of Serampore, lived in Kashi in his ripe old age. He was a devout person who would go to see Trailanga Swami every day with some fruits and pure milk as offerings for the Swami.

He felt that his life had become meaningful with the grace of the Swami. One day, he felt peculiar palpitations and became tense and anxious wondering if there was anything wrong that had happened with his family in Serampore.

Swamiji watched his anxiety and consoled him and reassured him by saying, "*Just wait for sometime, I am going to find out and inform you about the actual state of your family.*" He asked Joy Gopal to return to him at dusk, without informing him of what he already knew through meditation. When Joy Gopal came at dusk to his place, Trailanga Swami said, "*My son, your eldest son is no more in this world. He had cholera and died this morning at 6 am. You will see him in your dream this night.*"

Joy Gopal believed him and began to lament bitterly, but he was consoled by the soothing words of the great yogi who made him realise that life is but ephemeral. Joy Gopal received the unfortunate news the next day by telegram and for him that confirmed once again the greatness of Swamiji.

Now we have to realise that Supreme Consciousness is omniscient and thus great sages can find out anything they want by accessing it through deep meditation, and without the aid of any communication tools like telegraph and without leaving their seats.

Whether it is in earthly or divine realms, they can access it through their subtle perception. Scientific progress and human greed will inevitably bring about calamity and destruction for life on this earth and then only then will the reconstruction and establishment of spirituality and truth will be possible. We can see that from the past too, as scientific progress led many societies to utter ruin after they had attained the very zenith of success, and likewise the present age will also reach the same destination. Hence we can conclude that the world and human life on this earth is essentially moving along two contra circular movements—progress and regress. These movements are irresistible and eternal.

॥ ॐ तत् सत् ॥

|| om tat sat ||

Chapter 6. Trailanga Swami—Beyond doubts

With his *sadhana* at its very peak, Trailanga Swami was perpetually in union with the Supreme Consciousness.

In this state, an ascetic is supposed to have transcended beyond the three *gunas* (operational principle or tendency)—that is, *sattva* (balance, purity), *rajas* (dynamism, movement) and *tamas* (negativity, lethargy) that characterise all natural phenomena. In this state, he is not bound by any human limitations enforced by the perceptions of the physical senses and is beyond any psychological limitations.

His mind had transcended his body and was in complete control such that the extremities of summer or winter made no difference to him whatsoever. He was completely at peace while resting on a stone slab under the scorching heat of the summer mid-day. Seeing him lying on the hot sands of Kashi once, Shri Ramakrishna Paramahamsa had exclaimed: "*I saw that the Universal Lord Himself was using his body as a vehicle for manifestation. He was in an exalted state of knowledge. There was no body consciousness in him. The sand there had become so hot that no one could set foot on it. But he lay comfortably on it.*"

Likewise, biting cold weather made no difference either. Quite often, he used to immerse his body into ice-cold water and stay there for long periods of meditation. Sometimes, he was seen floating against the current like a fish. At other times, he used only one blanket during winter, though he never bothered about any creature comfort at all and preferred to remain unclad and uncovered.

Most of the times, he would be seen deeply absorbed in meditation. Even in public interactions, he was a dweller of his own inner world. He was completely indifferent to earthly affairs. No sign of any emotion was evident on his face, and he seemed to be in the state of perfect tranquility, frequently described as *sat-chit-ananda* (existence-knowledge-bliss). His primary purpose to exist upon earth appeared solely to provide the suffering humanity grace through his sacred and blissful presence.

He was apathetic to food and never sought his next meal. He had taken a vow of *ayachaka*—non-seeking—remaining satisfied with whatever he received. He took rice, bread, fruits—whatever was offered to him, without any complaints. Even the quantity of food that he consumed was not regular or fixed. Whether he was eating one *seer* (a unit of weight in the Indian subcontinent—approximately 2 pounds) or forty *seers* of food, it made no difference to him. Once, Shri Ramakrishna Paramahamsa fed him twenty *seers* of *kheer* (rice pudding) with his own hands. On the other hand, he used to fast for months without any apparent ill-effects.

Once a few sceptics determinded to expose the Mahaguru as a fraud and brought a mixture of lime and water in a bucket and offered it to him as milk. The omniscient Swamiji consumed the mixture without saying anything and there was no reaction on his peaceful face. The bewildered sceptics fell at the Swamiji's feet and started begging for mercy. Trailanga Swami, who was calm and quiet throughout, urinated what he had ingested, and the people assembled saw that lime and water had come out separately. Eyes wide open with shock, the rogues ran away. They paid for their sins and died very soon after the incident.

Injustice, harm, or oppression to spiritual aspirants and sadhus is never allowed by God. If one touches fire, it burns the hand. There were devout people ranging from the rich to the poor who flocked to him and made offerings of valuable garments or such like at his feet, as a token of their worship.

But once they left, money-minded louts rushed in and plundered anything they perceived as valuable from him. Swamiji never resisted or stopped them, exemplifying the real meaning of the saying, "*Sona O maati, sama gyaan*" (there's no discrimination, whether it be gold or mud).

Once, Trailanga Swami was passing by the royal palace of Vizianagram, accompanied by the great sage Mahatma Vijaykrishna Goswami. He paused there for a few moments as the palace guards fell at his feet seeking blessings. The king, too, came out hurrying when he heard about the Swami's presence, and requested them with devotion to grace his royal chambers. He looked at Vijaykrishna but the latter did not accompany Trailanga Swami. Swamiji was adorned with valuable robes and golden ornaments on his arm, waist, head etc. But when he came out of the palace, some local goons robbed the Swamiji of all those posessions. However, the palace guards caught them red handed. The king rushed out and saw the Swamiji in the same peaceful state that he always was in. The king was wise enough. He said, "*Those gifts are now your own—I don't have any right to take any action for them.*" Swamiji said to him, pointing to the robbers, "*They could change nothing within me. I am always in the same state anywhere, one that of a mendicant, by God's grace.*" As per the Swamiji's wishes, the miscreants were let free and Swamiji also left the place. Everybody there was perplexed, but they definitely perceived the divine within the Maha Yogi.

Nudity in public is a punishable offence in the British Court of Law. The British administration does not allow any grown-up man to remain unclad in public. But Trailanga Swami was an exception. We all know that thousands of unclad Naga sadhus (naked sages) descend from their caves in the Himalayan ranges during the Kumbha Mela to take holy dip in the sacred rivers since ages. People from all parts of the world assemble there, and the Nagas don't face any legal obstruction at these fairs.

During the days of British rule in India, many Englishmen used to visit the holy city of Kashi. The women among these Britishers would become quite embarrassed on noticing the naked men as they were not used to seeing such things in their own countries. During such a period, a particularly strict magistrate warned Swamiji to stop his nudity in public, but the Swamiji did not pay any attention.

One day, he was usually sitting on the sands of the Ganges, when a policeman ordered him to come with him to the police station. When Trailanga Swami did not respond, the policeman felt insulted and struck him with his cane. The crowd there started resisting the policeman and he became angry and informed his superiors. Immediately, other policemen rushed over and arrested the Swamiji. He was duly presented in the court of law the next day. The British judge presiding warned Swamiji and forbade him from staying naked anymore. Swamiji said nothing, and at this, the British officer became furious and ordered the police to put handcuffs on the Swamiji. To his utter bewilderment, Swamiji was no longer visible there! He had disappeared!

After a short while, they saw him standing near them with a smiling face. The competent lawyers hired by Swamiji's disciples explained to the officer that the sage standing before his eyes was beyond the normal social etiquette. They explained to the officer that for the Swamiji, human waste and a piece of sandalwood were identical; that he is a *sanyasi* who has transcended all mundane rules and regulations and one who does not require any apparel to wear.

Having listened, the arrogant British officer asked if the Swamiji would eat a meal offered by him. To this, the Swamiji responded by asking the officer the same question. The officer assumed that the Swami would offer him the usual food of sadhus i.e. fruits, milk, bread etc. He agreed to do so, at which point, the Swamiji evacuated his bowels on his own palm and offered the excreta to the officer.

The British officer was shocked and declined to eat Swamiji's waste as food. Then, before a dumbfounded assembly of people, Trailanga Swami poured the content of his hands into his own mouth and instantly the place became full of the fragrance of sandalwood. The bewildered British officer decided to allow him to remain unclad in public and go wherever he wanted thereafter.

After this particular officer got transferred, a new magistrate, who was more arrogant than his colleague, took over. One day, he also became agitated on seeing the Swamiji unclad when he was on his way going somewhere with his wife. He immediately got the Swamiji locked up in police custody. The next morning, he was informed that though the lock of the cell in which Swamiji was kept was intact, somehow the prisoner had come out of the cell.

He rushed out and saw the sage walking on the floor of the verandah completely unperturbed. He asked the Swamiji as to how he freed himself. The Swamiji replied that at dawn he felt like coming outside from the dark cell and so he came out.The officer carefully examined the lock and then saw water on the floor of the prison.

On being asked as to what that was, Swamiji informed him that it was his urine. The officer got upset and again imprisoned the Swamiji, but this time in a double locked cell and went back to his court room.

A few minutes later he saw the prisoner standing in the court room with a benign smile on his face. Swamiji said, "*No one could be imprisoned for perpetuity within a prison cell; if that was indeed possible, man would have been immortal.*"

The completely bewildered British officer again asked him as to how on earth it was possible for him to come out of the cell. Swamiji replied by explaining that the human body is mortal and without any strength of its own, but that it is the soul, the consciousness, that does not find anything to be impossible, and then said, "*My son! You too do not have the power of your own; why then are you oppressing me in this way?*"

The officer issued an order to his men never to bother the saint in future.

Let us realise the truth that spiritual powers can overpower any mundane problem. Swamiji clearly demonstrated this truth on that day. Let us also sing the glories of the magnanimity of the Supreme Entity! Exclaim "God is almighy!" Truth triumphs in the long run! Justice triumphs in the long run! God is the other name of truth!

॥ ॐ तत् सत् ॥

|| om tat sat ||

Chapter 7. At the courtyard of Mangal Bhattji

In 1800 Swamiji moved locations where he pursued his spiritual practices from the Dashaswamedh Ghat and settled on the *ghat* of Pancha Ganga near the twin flag of Bindu Madhav.

After staying there for seven years, he was taken to a separate residence dedicated for the Swamiji by a Marathi devotee of his, who arranged for all that the Swamiji required for his *sadhana* without him being disturbed in any way possible.

The owner of the house Mangal Bhattji, his old mother Amba Devi and younger brothers Mahadev Bhattji and Krishna Bhatt offered their service to the Guru with sincere devotion and ensured that he could continue his spiritual pursuits peacefully. Swamiji also graced them by staying there for a long period of eighty years without any break all the way up to his *Mahasamadhi* (act of consciously and intentionally leaving one's body, especially in the case of englightened beings).

It is indeed rare in history to see such devout disciples who served their Guru for such a long period of time and that too at an unbroken stretch. It was verily the epitome of devotion and dedication to the Guru! In Hindi, people say: "*Guru ki sewa se bhagwan mile*"—service to Guru begets the grace of God,

Swamiji took the vow of silence before he was taken to the place of Mangal Bhattji, but when the tales of his spiritual powers spread among the populace, inquisitive crowds began to gather. Having been disturbed, Swamiji kept total silence except one night in a week, when he spoke to his disciples. In order to respond to spiritual aspirants who came to him with their questions, he adopted a method of providing concise hints. Mangal Bhattji, due to his constant proximity to Swamiji, over time was able to decipher the meaning of these hints.

In those days, Swamiji used to be usually lying down on a high altar. Many *shlokas* (holy verses) were inscribed on the surrounding walls in Devnagari script. So whenever some one asked some religious or spiritual question, he used to point to the letters on the walls and Mangal Bhattji used to write them down accordingly on a piece of paper.

Once the answer was complete, Mangal Bhattji read them out for the benefit of the person putting forth the question. The words 'promulgation' and 'preacher' are essentially ideas and concepts from the western world. They don't quite capture the real essence of what the Guru is trying to teach their disciples, and the process becomes somewhat mechanical. It is safe to assume that many such Gurus are not well qualified to teach real lessons to their disciples. Shri Ramakrishna Paramahamsa used to refer to such Gurus as '*chaprash heen*' (a person without the badge indicating authority). People naturally obey and do not doubt anyone holding an official badge of a government entity. Without the official badge, however, no one pays any attention to them.

We like to opine here that recitation of the texts from the *shastras*, learning them by rote without realising the truth within, does not help much. Similarly, even the listeners may not be competent enough to understand and realize the message of the Guru; and they may very well be insincere as well. Such people also are deprived of the real essence of teachings from their Gurus.

Savvy people know better than to trust unknown merchants or hawkers and so avoid their goods of dubious quality. Likewise, smart people with spiritual inclination do not accept messages from unknown preachers.

Like the buyers who go to stores with a reputation for quality, people in India seeking eternal emancipation go to seek it from the saints and sadhus who are known to be already emancipated by the grace of the Eternal God.

But such Gurus are not seen going door to door to cater salvation to the masses; instead, the aspirants go to them, abide by their messages and achieve eternal salvation. Good and noble company always pays, and this has been true for time immemorial. We accumulate bad karma by doing unjust, impure deeds over multiple births including in the present life. Such karma can only be washed off by the sincere devotion to God, good company, sincere efforts to improve and constant search for truth.

The *rishis say*: "God is like a *Kalpataru*" (a tree that fulfills each and every desire). A devout honest soul can be granted with all the four *purusharthas* (objectives of a human existence) by God's grace, viz. 1) *dharma* (righteousness) 2) *artha* (wealth) 3) *kama* (desire) 4) *moksha* (salvation).

Swamiji used to often cite quotes like, "*A lotus can easily be located by its own fragrance*", "*Teaching by example is better than preaching*", and "*Ideology based on Truth is the greatest*".

He noted that from our history it is obvious that hundreds of thousands of good souls became pious and spiritually inclined from the inspiration and example set by many great sages. This is similar to how a flame from a single lamp can kindle countless lamps, and how a single seed of a banyan tree yields countless banyan trees. A banyan tree is always there in the womb of its single seed.

Trailanga Swamiji thus graced countless lives with his spiritual presence and advice even though he was observing a vow of silence for many years of his existence on earth.

In our humble opinion, no amount of praise does justice to the lives of such great saints. Once, Shri Ramakrishna Paramhamsa said to Rakhal Maharaj: "*A certain man went to Trailanga Swami. He watched him silently and thought he would get nothing from him to satisfy his desires. On another day, when he visited Swamiji's place, he saw him weeping bitterly and simultaneously bursting in laughter. The man realised deep in his heart that God can be attained only when one comes to yearn as sincerely deep within for the grace of God.*"

("Dharma Prasange"—Swami Brahmananda)

This is an example how being in the presence of spiritual greatness can have a wonderful impact on a person! With his abilities to perceive the deepest thoughts of people, Trailanga Swami could dispel doubts in visitors assembled at his place, and even address complicated queries that people had in their spiritual pursuits. When we are in the proximity of each other, we can exchange views and understand each other easily. But spiritually exalted saints can figure those things out even if they are far away. The first two *shlokas* of the Guru Stotram reads thus:

अखण्ड-मण्डलाकारं व्याप्तं येन चराचरम्

तत्पदम् दर्शितं येन तस्मै श्री गुरवे नमः ॥

akhaṇḍa-maṇḍalākāraṁ vyāptaṁ yena carācaram
tatpadam darśitaṁ yena tasmai śrī gurave namaḥ ||

Translation: *My Salutations to that Guru who revealed to me that Truth, which is unfragmented, infinite, timeless divinity, and which pervades the entire universe—movable or unmovable.*

अज्ञान तिमिरान्धस्य ज्ञानाञ्जन शलाकया

चक्शुरुन्मीलितं येन तस्मै श्री गुरवे नमः ॥

ajñāna timirāndhasya jñānājana śalākaya
cakśurunmilītaṁ yena tasmai śrī gurave namaḥ ||

Translation: *My salutations to that reverential Guru, who opened my eyes, by applying the divine collyrium of self-knowledge in my eyes, which had become blind by the cataract of ignorance.*

The graceful silent saint thus saved countless men from the normal pursuit of material and sensory pleasures, countless irascible and hard-hearted men became kind and compassionate devotees, countless people suffering from physical ailments got relief by his grace.

At times saints and pandits from many other places came to him to resolve their problems and with questions around spiritual pursuits.

Trailanga Swami had written down about 30 manuscripts with his own hand. Whenever needed, he used to bring them out to solve knotty questions/problems presented to him. Usually at dusk, some sadhus would come to him for his counsel and opinions on questions put forth by them.

At times he broke his vow of silence to deliver his opinions. For instance, on the occasion of giving *mantra deeksha* to the late Mahatma Vijaykrishna Goswami, he broke his silence and delivered a few words in sermon.

We know he lived under the bare sky during the last phase of his life at the courtyard of Mangal Bhattji, as he did not establish any permanent dwelling place or an ashram. A large statue of Trailanga Swami, carved out of black stone, was installed when he was at Kashi, and afterwards another black statue was installed on the altar in the north of the courtyard of Bhattji's residence after his departure.

Next to his sacred statue, there is a large idol of Maha Kali along with a large *Shivalinga* on the western side. At the southern part of the courtyard, an idol of Beni Madhav can be found. All these three idols were installed with a ritual called *Praana Pratishtha* (invoking of the divine energy) performed by Swamiji himself.

What is noteworthy is that the Kali idol is unusual in the sense the tongue of the Goddess is not sticking out as is usually the depiction, and nor is there a supine Shiva at her feet. Depiction in this form is referred to as '*Mangal Gouri Maa*'. It is said that having been advised by an astrologer, Swamiji brought out those idols from under the Ganges water and installed them with his own hands in the courtyard of Mangal Bhattji.

This *Shivalinga* has recently become a popular pilgrimage destination in the name of '*Traila Nageshwara Shiva*'. A room where he used to perform his spiritual austeries or *sadhana* for years is still present located under the statue of Trailanga Swami. Swamiji used to give his disciples *mantra deeksha* in that room.

The only living disciple of Swamiji, the holy Shri Shri Shankari Mataji, a celibate, was also given *mantra deeksha* by her Guru Trailanga Swami in that room when she was twelve years old. She continued her *sadhana* for another 12 years in that same room.

For all these reasons the residence of Mangal Bhattji became famous as the *math* (ashram) of Trailanga Swami, to the extent that there is a signboard hung on the outer wall by the residents of the ashram. Trailanga Swami himself never established any ashram or *math,* did not worry about any impermanent things of this nature or seek any fancy title. Unshackled by any such affairs and unmoved by words of praise, he was completely free of matters mundane.

His life was wonderful, sacred and worthy enough to be regarded as one of the greatest saints that this world had ever seen, one who set alight the sacred flames of true religion—truth above all.

॥ ॐ तत् सत् ॥

|| om tat sat ||

Chapter 8. Mahasamadhi and disappearance of Trailanga Swami

Waves rising, breaking and eventually dying out are a frequent occurence in the seas, and this has been happening incessantly since time immemorial. Although we can observe the rising of waves one after the other before merging into the vastness of the ocean, we cannot specifically identify a single wave or differentiate it in particular from the rest. The life of a man in the sea of eternity is similar—he is born and then goes at the completion of his role on earth. Trailanga Swami was born on earth during the period of Muslim rule in India, and it ended during the British rule.

In 1883, Swamiji informed a few of his disciples that he would embark on his final journey after about 5 years. Eventually that time arrived. In the year 1294 (AD1887), in the month of *Agrahayan*, he disclosed to his disciples that he will get emanicipated on his birthday towards the end of the month.

He was in perfect health and possessed a body unafflicted by any disease. He was not at all weakened or impaired by age, neither physically nor psychologically, and that was because he was able to control '*Ashta Prakriti*'—the eight limbs of existence, due to the powers he had accumulated through intense *sadhana*.

The news spread like fire that the *Bhishma* of *Kaliyuga* would be voluntarily leaving his body soon. All the disciples, devotees, sadhus and *paramahamsas* rushed towards Kashi, to try and see him in person for the last time before his emancipation. A great bustle descended on the city, with swarms of people like surging waves reaching to have a final *darshan* of the great Swamiji.

The month was coming to its end gradually, and there were only ten days left. Kalikananda Swami, Sadananda Swami, Brahmananda Swami,

Bholananda Swami, Brahmashri Mangal Bhattji, Amba Devi, Ambalika Devi, Shri Shri Shankari Mataji, and Shri Umacharan Mukhopadhyay were among the disciples and devotees present to witness the final journey of the great saint.

The affectionate Swamiji began to enrich them further by giving them spiritual advice and guidance. They had the great privilege of quenching their spiritual thirst and aspirations of realising the Supreme Reality from one who had realised it himself.

The epitome of wisdom, Trailanga Swami, addressed their queries around complex problems they had run into, during their own spiritual pursuits. Similarly, other religious people and spiritually rich sadhus got the answers they needed from Swamiji and left the place after paying their respects to the Swami.

One day before his final journey, Trailanga Swami instructed his disciples to procure a stone chest that could accommodate him in seated position. He told them to place his body in the chest after his demise and lock it up, and instructed that they submerge the stone chest in the waters of the Ganges near the Pancha Ganga Ghat and in front of the Adi Sanyasi Guru Dattatreya temple, but without performing any funeral rites.

He finally told his disciples: "*Place the stone chest across two boats that are next to each other, and row them up to Asi Ghat and then up to the river Varuna, and finally push the chest overboard in the middle of the Ganges in front of the Adi Dattatreya Temple.*"

Then he informed everyone that he would soon resume his vow of silence, and said, "*If you would like to ask me anything, ask it soon.*"

For the reader's benefit, we would like to state that since the ancient times, *jala samadhi* (water burial) has been the traditional way of disposing of the physical bodies of saints. That being said, burial under soil is also a common practice in Kashi, with quite a few memorial temples over burial spots present. It is also said that Shri Ramachandra, the 7th avatar of Lord Vishnu, chose a water-burial in the Sarayu River during the *Treta Yuga*.

Quite a few people asked Swamiji the questions they had, and he replied to them later in the night. Swamiji gave instructions to his disciple Shri Shri Shankari Mataji, whom he had kept with him in the ashram, and gave *upadesha* (sacred advice) to visit famous pilgrimage centres after his *Mahasamadhi* and explained the duties she needed to undertake in the future.

He emphasised that he would always be present in his subtle body. Shri Shri Mataji wept at his holy feet, and with a heavy heart accepted the advice and duties as his blessing. She subsequently lived in various parts of India as an itinerant *sanyasin*.

In a subsequent chapter we are going to provide a short biography of her holy life, and the invaluable advice she gave, and additionally go over the details of her life as a *sanyasin*. Her disciples and devotees recently established a Bhajan Ashram, on 10th Chaitra in 1939, in Kashi at 142, Audhgarbhi area (near Harish Chandra Ghat Road).

Shri Umacharan Mukherji, one of the Bengali disciples of Swamiji, also knelt down before his Guru and asked him that what was going to be his ultimate fate. Swamiji said, "*Umacharan, my son! Do not forsake your duties. You should continue to do your present duties but do not leave the 'Khunti' (the post).*" Swamiji was referring to God allegorically as '*Khunti*', or the post to be attached to. If one retains attachment to God, one is free from ailments of life.

The stone chest was made as per Swamiji's instructions. Within the chest, a bed was created with raised cushions, pillows and a bed cover. Flower bunches, garlands, sandalwood accessories were added to embellish. The boats were kept ready.

The next morning, at 8 a.m., Swamiji entered the small room under his altar where he used to perform his spiritual austerities. Sitting on the *asana* (seat), he said to his disciples, "*My dear children! Please shut the door and do not open it till you do hear me knocking on it.*" The disciples shut the door and waited there expectantly.

At about 3 p.m., there was the knock on the door and it was opened by the sad disciples. Swamiji came out and stood on the verandah. He gestured that the chest be taken towards Pancha Ganga. When it was done, Trailanga Swami sat within, in a yogic posture. The chest was then locked up as per his instructions.

At that point, a wonderful sight was seen, as if celestial effulgence was emanating from within the chest.

It was the winter month of *Poush*, and the eleventh day of the fortnight with the waxing moon in the fourth lunar asterism *Rohini*, December 1887. On that day, just prior to the impending sunset, and at an age of 280 years Trailanga Swami entered *Mahasamadhi* by means of *Agni Yoga* and merged into the Supreme.

With this event, one of the brightest stars from the sky of Indian spiritual history, the living Vishwanath Himself of the holy city of Kashi, disappeared into the ocean of eternity.

The news of his departure spread fast, and countless people thronged the *ghats* of Kashi to pay their respects. The number of people was similar to the teeming masses that gather since time immemorial with the intent of taking a holy dip in the sacred water of the Ganges on particularly auspicious occasions like *Varuni Yoga* (the thirteenth lunar day of the dark fortnight in the month of Chaitra), *Churamoni Yoga* (a rare astronomical combination considered to be highly auspicious by Hindus), *Ardhodaya Yoga* (a particularly auspicious combination of the sun with a star). These rituals are still very prevalent in India, performed with intense devotional fervor.

We can realise from this as to how lessons imparted by the great *rishis* and *munis* have penetrated deep into the very core of our Indian way of life. By their grace, hundreds of sages and saints take birth in India to guide the life of the seekers towards the zenith of spiritual development.

India has been blessed by the presence of innumerable saints on its soil who provide solace and spiritual guidance to its people.

We find peace and bliss while in the proximity of these saints, and enrich ourselves; and when they depart we become sad but not weak, because they gave us the eternal message that divine truth is forever real. Separations happen temporarily, but it only validates that the soul is eternal and beyond space and time.

The ten customary rituals prescribed to householders under *Sanatana Dharma* have had a great and important impact on our tradition and culture, in a way that is perhaps matchless in the world. What do we understand from the name *Bharat Varsha*? For the benefit of our dear readers, we will attempt to explain it as follows:

भारत वर्श	=	भा रत वर्श
bhārata varśa		bhā rata varśa

"bhā = *Ray of light or the efflulgent light of the Sun, True Knowledge or knowledge of Truth, the Absolute God*".

This refers to the insight or the wisdom required for perceiving the Supreme Reality, and the power to realise the meaning of the proverb.

सर्वं खल्विदम् ब्रह्म

sarvaṁ khalvidam brahma

Translation: *All this is verily Brahman.*

This should not just be understood theoretically, but one should perceive it through *sadhana* and via true wisdom gained, thus penetrating those transluscent depths of *maya*. Those who are incessantly '**rata**', or engaged in a 'union' with the Divine, dwell in *Bharat Varsha*. This is why we say that our dear motherland is indeed a land blessed by God, and a land full of spiritual riches.

So we repeat our appeal to you, dear reader, to make an attempt to know the extent and understand the spiritual wisdom present in India, where all of us believe in the re-emergence of eternal soul.

This belief is firmly based on the knowledge of the Law of Karma, which states that the form of an animated being in succeeding lives solely depends on the deeds of its previous lives on earth. One can reincarnate in various forms during one's progression. This, in turn, depends on the inner transformation of the soul with respect to the *trigunas—sattva*, *tamas*, and *rajas*.

These *gunas* are the three parts of the *Saguna Brahman*, or *The Absolute with qualities,* or the *manifested* Divine. Man thus has to take part in this cycle of life and death, birth, and re-emergence. The achievement of insight required to attain the knowledge of '*Poorna Satya*' (Complete Truth), is prevalent only in India; this therefore confirms the success of '*Brahmacharya*'—the devotional austerities, *sadhana* and inquisitiveness to know the Supreme *Brahman*.

'*Brahmacharya'* has two modes: (1) *Khanda Brahmacharya*, or spiritual pursuits on a part-time basis, and (2) *Akhanda Brahmacharya*, which stands for complete absorption in *sadhana* and austerities. Without the practice of *Brahmacharya*, we are depriving ourselves of the strength and merit of *Brahmacharya* everyday and becoming weaker. Let us ignite the holy flame of fire—to seek God with sincere desire in our hearts and thus remove any weaknesses of the mind, and regain the supreme felicity and peace even while living this ephemeral life.

May God bestow us with truth, devotion, and love. Obviously His Grace is with us through all the scriptural texts and practices. But on our part, it is our duty to uplift our mind and soul and realize the meaning of '*Manushya*'—human-consciousness, and work towards being worthy of the grace of God and other God-like saints. Only then we can get respite from earthly ailments, woes and worries, maladies and reach the Divine.

Following his instructions, the sacred body of Shri Trailanga Swami was duly adorned with flowers, garlands and sandalwood paste. It was then placed in the chest on the last bed of the boat.

The boat then sailed towards the Asi Ghat. The banks of all the 84 *ghats* were densely crowded. People thronged there to witness the water burial of the great saint.

Cries of sorrow and the wailing from the crowd made the atmosphere mournful, though it was only a spontaneous reaction out of the crowd expressing their grief. The boat sailed from Asi Ghat to the north towards the famous Pancha Ganga Ghat in front of the Dattatreya Temple.

The yogi once again displayed his supernatural powers to help his disciples, who, while attempting to immerse the stone chest felt that it was almost weightless as if empty. At this, some wanted to see the Mahayogi once again for the last time. After a discussion, they opened the stone chest and to their astonishment found it empty! Only a mass of flowers was there! With a heart full of sorrow, they immersed the stone chest into the river, and the crowd dispersed gradually thereafter.

The *shastras* (scriptures) say that great saints who embrace death at their own will, convert their mortal body into a heap of ashes. But Bhagwan Shri Krishna was an exception; as the Shrimad Bhagavat Purana says:

लोकाभिरामां स्व-तनुं धारण-ध्यान-मंगलम्

योग-धारणयग्नेय्या-दग्ध्वा धामाविशत् स्वकम् ॥

lokābhirāmāṁ sva-tanuṁ dhāraṇa-dhyāna-maṁgalam
yoga-dhāraṇayagneyyā-dagdhvā dhāmāviśat svakam
(Shrimad Bhagavatam, 11.31.6)

Translation: *Without employing the mystic Agni Yoga to burn up His transcendental body, Lord Kṛṣṇa entered into His own abode.*

(2) The great devotee Dhruva also entered the heaven in this way as per Shrimad Bhagavatam, Canto 4.

(3) Mahaprabhu Shri Shri Chaitanya Dev departed from the holy Jagannath in Puri without giving up his mortal body. He was seen among

seven *kirtan* groups at the same time he disappeared! According to popular belief, the holy body of Mahaprabhu Shri Shri Chaitanyadev merged into the idol of Lord Jagannatha or into the broken thigh of Tota Gopinath.

(4) King Yudhishthira also became immortal in the area Satpath in the Himalayas. The place is situated above Badrikashram or Badrinarayan Dham.

(5) The famous queen devotee Meerabai, who renounced family life, went to the holy Vrindavan Dham in the last stage of her life. She received *mantra deeksha* from her Guru Shri Shri Jiv Goswami and finally she also disappeared, merging into her guardian deity Giridharji or Shri Krishna.

(6&7) Similar stories about Mahatma Kabir and the famous hero of Chittor, Bappa Rao, are well known.

(8) There are many other such exemplary events that have taken place in our holy motherland since ages. The holy city of *Varanasi* is located at the confluence of two rivers *Varuna* and *Asi*.

The Mahayogi left his body at his own will from that place, but for him it was nothing unnatural. No malady or affliction had tamed him for even a single moment in his long life of 280 years. He lived strong, and devoted his existence to purely pursuing spiritual progress in an uninterrupted manner. He could stay under the water of the Ganges for hours. The British prisons could not restrain him and he used to disappear frequently and whenever he desired, and he had revived many corpses or brought dying people back to life with his grace. So there is question that he disappeared after giving up his mortal body in front of the bewildered eyes of mournful crowd.

A Protest

Most ruefully, we would like to lodge our protest against dubious rumours that have spread wide pertaining to the demise of the great Trailanga

Swami. We feel it is our duty to address these individually, and hope that our dear readers realise our intention in doing so. The rumours:

(1) Trailanga Swami had become obese and was suffering from gout. Further, because people considered him to be a living Shiva and poured milk and water on his head continuously from dawn to noon as *abhisheka*, especially in the winter months of *Poush* and *Magha*, he had developed septic sores all over his body. Having been in such a painful state for quite some time, he left his earthly presence and then was buried under the waters of the Ganges.

(The Late Kuladananda Brahmachari / Shri Shri Sadguru Sanga 2nd part, P-97)

Many of us are aware of the fact that Trailanga Swami left his body in Bengali month *Pousha* (December 1887) in Kashi—that's almost a year after Shri Shri Thakur Ramakrishna Paramahamsa, who left his body in the Bengali month of *Shravana* (August 15, 1886).

Some of his contemporaries who were eye-witnesses to the event are still alive among us today, and they have no doubts regarding the real facts around the demise of Swamiji. It is indeed their fortune that they could see the holy event, and the Swami had himself foretold everything about his final journey leaving this impermanent body, in detail. He had even announced the exact day or '*tithi*' (the thirtieth part of the whole lunar month), position of the moon under the lunar asterism (*nakshatra*) *Rohini* when he would shed his mortal coil through *Agni Yoga* well in advance—5 months before the event.

Our beloved spiritual mother Shri Shri Shankari Mataji lived 61 years of her holy life in the proximity of her spiritual father Trailanga Swami. Born and brought up in Kashi, Mataji never saw her Guru afflicted by any disease. The late Umacharan Mukhopadhyay, one of Swamiji's disciples, also mentioned the truth about his Guru's demise in the biography of his Guru that he authored.

He was beyond any mortal limitations, and never suffered from any malady during the incredibly long life span of 280 years. The visitors as well as local people in Kashidham saw him regularly up to his age of 150 years. He was always stout and healthy.

Trailanga Swami passed the last part of his life, a span of 80 years, in the courtyard of his devout Marathi disciple and celibate Shri Mangal Bhattji. He had the fortune to serve his Guru with his own hands. Swamiji used to sit on an altar and after taking his *darshan*, nobody was allowed to come close and stand there for much time. They had to salute him from a distance and leave the place. He was always attended and served by his disciples like Mangal Bhattji himself, his brothers Mahadev and Ram Bhatt, Amba Devi, Ambalika Devi, and Shri Shri Mataji Shankari Devi. Nobody could visit Swamiji without their permission and thus it was impossible for anybody to pour milk and water on Swamiji's head continuously from containers.

It is strange that such claims are made in the name of Shri Vijaykrishna Goswami by the late Kuladananda Brahmachari. We can never believe that such statements were delivered by the venerable sage Vijaykrishna Prabhu himself. Even if he uttered them, it is obvious that he had been misled or perhaps had some misconception. We believe firmly that responsibility should go to the author or any of his representatives.

We would like to mention that the readers of the books "*Asha Bateer Upakhyan*" an excellent one written by Shri Vijaykrishna Goswami, or the large biography of Vijaykrishna "*Goswamijir Jeevanee*" authored by Shri Amritalal Sengupta, must know the extent of Vijaykrishna's reverence for Trailanga Swami.

He was also initially a disciple of Trailanga Swamiji, who gave him *upadesha* and introduced him to various aspects of spiritualism. Goswamiji's disciples, who are still living, will recount an interesting incident from his past, through which we know that Trailanga Swamiji once saved Goswamiji's life during his stay in Kumbha Mela. Trailanga Swami took the appearance of a little boy and rescued his dear disciple; and later on Goswamiji had come to know that the little boy who rescued him was none other that Trailanga Swamiji. (ref: Biography authored by Amritalal Sengupta)

Now it is the duty of discerning readers to judge for themselves this quote with an impartial eye and seek out the truth. Was it really possible by Goswamiji to pass such a remark about his first and foremost Guru? The speaker was Goswamiji, a great saint himself, and the subject of his comment was none other than Trailanga Swami. And the author, who in all likelihood inserted such a remark in Goswamiji's name, was also a *brahmachari* sage! We can only exclaim, "What foolishness!!!"

(2) Now we are citing below some incorrect statements that have been made in the biography tilted "*Mahatma Trailanga Swamir Jeevan Charitra*", authored by Shri Umacharan Mukhopadhyay.

a) In Bengali, the narration in the 7th and 8th lines at page no. 86 reads as follows:

"*Dehilam purber mato (p85 / 2nd line) Sabi thik ache. Kebal jihabe bahire naai, Ebong padatale Mahadev naai*"

I saw everything was intact as before, only the tongue was not visible and Mahadev was absent in front of the feet...

Here, the word *kebal* is only incorrect but the rest is well written. We have to omit the word '*kebal*' to interpret things correctly.

2) In the above mentioned biography by Umacharan (Page 101, 3rd line) we find a statement attributed to Trailanga Swami as "*Ami panchti shishya kariyachi*". **(Glossary 21)**.

This statement in the name of Trailanga Swami is not correct. Though he allowed very few to become his disciples, the fact is that he had at least twenty disciples, as stated by Shri Shri Mata Shankariji. You will find the full list of them in our book.

We guess here that Umacharan himself knew only of five of his *gurubhais* and was close to them. But he perhaps never came across his other *gurubhais* in his lifetime and therefore was misinformed. Further, on page 82 of the same book in the 1st and 2nd lines, he wrote:

"*Tanhar (samijir) dikshita hoibo bhabiya jeevanke dhanyo mone korilam. Aagami kalyo deeksha diben boliyachen.*" (Glossary 2, 3)

Also on page 111 of his book, he names 7 disciples of Swamiji but excludes his own name from the list. So his statement about the names and number of disciples of Trailanga Swami is inconsistent and clearly inaccurate.

3) In Umacharan's books, some other factual errors are worth pointing out in order to correct them. The 2nd line of page 111 reads "*Ami shayan korite pari*" (Glossary 4), which translates to "*I can lie down*". It is completely wrong and should have been written as "*Ami upabeshan korite pari*" (Glossary 5), i.e. "*I can be seated*". This is because the sages or sadhus are buried under water or the earth keeping their body in seated position.

Again in the 9th line, page 113 the information "*Bedeer pPashe*" (Glossary 6), i.e. *beside the altar* is wrong, that should have been "*Bedir nimne*" (Glossary 7), i.e. *under the altar*. In the 20th and 21st line of the same page the statement "*Tanhake snduker bhitar bhalo bichanay shayan karaiya*" (Glossary 8), i.e. "*making him lie on a good bed*" is not correct, instead it should have been written as "*Bhalo aashane basaiya*" (Glossary 18), i.e. "*making him sit on a good seat*", instead of "*ichanay*" and "*shayan karaiya*".

All these incorrect details pertaining to Swamiji's demise might have been the result of Umacharan's ignorance while writing this portion of his book.

Was he confused? Let us go through another statement of his book (Page 92): "*El aakal ghatana jaha dekhile ebong sei sakal katha barta jaha sunile taha kono abishwashi loker nikat boliyo naa*". (Glossary 9).

His own feelings are described as (Page114): "*Hriday bidirno hoite lagilo, Dukkhe buk patiya jaite lLagilo, Eto diner par aami bal buddhi sakoli jaha kichu sakoli harailam*" (Glossary 10), which was completely true and real reflection of his grief at the *Mahasamadhi* of his own Guru. His erroneous statements, therefore, we believe, are the result of this condition of his mind affecting the required concentration of an author while recording history.

Under these circumstances, we would take the version of Trailanga Swamiji's *Manasaputri*, Shri Shri Shankari Mataji, as more authentic.

The author would most humbly like to draw the attention of the dear readers to other errors made in another book titled "Jeevanee Sangraha" by Shri Ganesh Chandra Mukhopadhyay. He said, "*Inhar bibaha korite adou ichha chilona, Kebol matar anurodhe bibaho koriya chilen.*" [(Glossary 11)], translated as *he was reluctant to marry, but did so to abide by his mother's request.*

This is also far from the truth. It is easy to understand that lack of his proximity to Swamiji's family is responsible for such misconceptions. Based on rumour and hearsay, he made such claims in his book.

Trailanga Swami remained a lifelong celibate, just like the four Kumaras (Sanaka, Sanandana, Sanatana, and Sanatkumara) and Narada Rishi—celibates since time immemorial who remained in the domain of God. Some other *rishis* adopted attachment to worldliness. The class of the *rishis* like Narada etc. is rare.

Shri Bhaskarananda Saraswati Swami, who was a contemporary to Trailanga Swami, was a family man in his first part of life and left his family life after the death of his wife to adopt the life of a *sanyasi.* His original name was Matiram Mishra (Brahmins while staying in Bengal as tradesmen adopted the last name Mishra) and originally lived in Kanpur in Uttar Pradesh.

This book under discussion said: "*Athaish Bachor Bayoshe Inhar Marti Biyog Hoy*"—*He became motherless at the age of 28*; whereas Trailanga Swami lost his mother Vidyavati Devi when he was 52 of age. This can be verified from a piece of paper inscribed with Swamiji's hand writing that he stored in a pipe made out of bamboo, as well as his own description about this to Shri Shri Shankari Mataji.

4) According to an inscription (Page 187) in "Sata Jeevanee" edited by Shri Chandi Charan Basak, it reads: "*Ini anichhaa satteo matar anurodhe nibaha karen O matar jibatdashay arthat atchollish bachor bayosh porjanto grihasrame thakiya sansar jatra nirbha karen*" [(Glossary 11)], translated as "*In spite of his reluctance, he married at the request of his mother and lived the life of a married man till his mother's demise when the Swamiji was forty eight*".

Here we see another statement that is completely untrue, and is probably written only based on rumour or hearsay.

Shri Shri Shankari Mataji lived almost her entire life in close proximity to her Guru Trailanga Swami. We are aware of the facts from listening to her sweet narration of the history of Swamiji's life.

It is our humble request to all of you to correct any such dubious statements if encountered anywhere, and by any means possible. I would like to take the responsibility of all such mistakes and request your pardon, and for this magnanimity, I shall remain ever grateful to you.

|| ॐ तत् सत् ||

|| om tat sat ||

Chapter 9. Trailanga Swami and his philosophy of the Shastras

A detailed study of Trailanga Swami's life and work reveals that he was the living embodiment of the messages proclaimed by God Himself as recorded in the holy Bhagavad Gita. Trailanga Swami came down to exemplify the well-known spiritual messages from the Gita that indicate that the upliftment of all and sundry is possible through spiritual activities, and through which one gets respite from the ailments of this epheremal life.

The omniscient God Lord Krishna conveyed His holy messages in response to Arjuna's confusion, moral dilemma and despondence, when the latter saw his kith and kin in the battle field of Kurukshetra standing against him as foes. To invigorate Arjuna's heroic and brave nature, Lord Krishna who was his charioteer in this battle, explains to Arjuna that he needs to do his duty as a warrior and prince, and elaborates on various qualities that should exist in a man.

The Bhagavad Gita, in chapters 2nd, 6th, 12th and 14th, contains these messages. The second chapter describes the indications of true wisdom, the 6th indicates the characteristics of a free soul, the 12th chapter describes the qualities of the Lord's favourite devotees and the 14th chapter contains the qualities of a man beyond the conventional physical attributes. All those qualities described, that of a soul free from the cycle of birth and death, were visible in the great sage Trailanga Swami in complete detail, almost as if the *shlokas* were written about the Swamiji himself.

Arjuna's Question

स्तिथप्रज्ञस्य का भाषा समाधिस्थस्य केशव।

स्थितधीः किं प्रभाषेत किमासीत व्रजेत किम्॥

stithaprajñasya kā bhāṣā samādhisthasya keśava |
sthitadhīḥ kiṁ prabhāṣeta kimāsīta vrajeta kim ||
(The Bhagavad Gita 2:54)

Translation: *What are the signs of one properly situated in perfect knowledge? Of one absorbed in pure spiritual consciousness? How does one steadfast in this consciousness talk? How does he sit? How does he walk?*

Arjuna asked four questions to Lord Krishna as narrated in the Gita:

Samādhisthasya of one absorbed in pure spiritual consciousness; **stithaprañasya** — of one situated properly in perfect knowledge

1) **kā bhāṣā** — what are the signs of one properly situated in perfect knowledge? Of one absorbed in pure spiritual consciousness?

2) **kiṁ prabhāṣeta** — How does one steadfast in this consciousness talk?

3) **kimāsīta** — How does he sit? And,

4) **vrajeta kim** — How does he walk?

It should also be observed keenly that how they get back to a 'normal' state from the depths of *samadhi* That's why it is opined that only the devoted souls could judge them perfectly, just like only a diamond-merchant can assess the true value of diamond.

The author would most humbly like to opine that only the ideology of such great souls should be followed. The loftier one's ideology is, the greater the height that one will reach.

प्रजहाति यदा कामान् सर्वान् पार्थ मनोगतान्।

आत्मन्येवात्मना तुष्टः स्थितप्रज्ञस्तदोच्यते॥

prajahāti yadā kāmān sarvān pārtha manogatān |
ātmanyevātmanā tuṣṭaḥ sthitaprajñastadocyate ||

(The Bhagavad Gita 2:55)

Translation: *When one gives up all desires for sensory gratification produced within the mind and becomes satisfied by the realisation of the Self in the pure state of the soul, then it is said one is properly situated in perfect knowledge.*

Lord Krishna describes the symptoms of truly self-realised people and opines that identifying such a person is near impossible from the external signs alone. The foremost indication of a truly self-realised person is the complete lack of all earthly desires, whether physical or mental. Because, till one's mind is overcome by earthly desires, one's mind cannot remain constantly focused on God.

Bhakti implies ardent yearning for God. It involves true and complete dedication of all the devotee's acts, whether physical or mental, towards God, the Supreme Entity. Attraction and attachment to matters mundane is the reason behind the instability of mind. No true wisdom or knowledge can be achieved without a mind that discriminates and a soul that is content.

One might argue that the very fulfillment or satisfaction of desires is the sole contributor to human pleasures; and that abstention of desires may be the source of all the misery in life. The Gita speaks the truth that the truly wise men are innately rich (*Antare tor dyakh cheye getha ananda niketan—Rabindranath Tagore*).

They are happy because their flute of life is hollow and thus the Divine flautist—the Supreme God—creates the melody of spirituality in them, so they do not have to depend on any external pleasures. They understand that satisfaction derived from worldly achievements is ephemeral and can only bring further misery. The truly wise persons, on the contrary, achieve perpetual peace of mind because they are happy within.

So let's examine whether the aforementioned symptoms of a self-realized person within the Gita are applicable to the life of Trailanga Swami.

What did young Shivaram do when he grew into a man in the prime of his health? He shunned inherited wealth, remained steadfast to the pleas and the love of a brother with the devotion of Lakshmana, sincere love and affection of his parents and rejected a proposed wife in the prime of her youth with ease, and with the complete detachment of a saint.

All temptations and lures were irrelevant in the face of Swamiji's detachment. He was completely indifferent to all the pleasures of temporal life, and was perpetually merged into the true and deep awareness of the formless Absolute. He became **ātmanyevātmanā tuṣṭaḥ**, i.e. by the realisation of the Self, he was in the pure state of the soul.

दुःखेष्वनुद्विग्नमनाः सुखेषु विगतस्पृहः।

वीतरागभयक्रोधः स्थितधीर्मुनिरुच्यते॥

duḥkheṣvanudvignamanāḥ sukheṣu vigataspṛahaḥ |
vītarāgabhayakrodhaḥ sthitadhīrmunirucyate ||
(The Bhagavad Gita 2:56)

Translation: *One whose mind is undisturbed by distress, without desires for happiness, free from attachment, fear and anger; that sage is known as steadfast in consciousness.*

Shri Krishna further expanded the attributes of one established truly in the Divine Self. Sudden tragedies or unexpected downturns in the life of a person usually lead to sorrow that is difficult to bear. One finds that it is hard to overcome and get respite from such situations. But under similar circumstences, the one who is established in the pure Self remains completely unhurt, shielded as he would be, by his usual detachment to all things mundane.

In his long life, no trouble could bother or distract Swamiji from his mission of life. Depraved men poured burning charcoal on his head when he was in a state of samadhi, others bothered and insulted him based on perceived affront to a queen's dignity. Her guards captured him by her order, and they lashed at him ruthlessly. But his complete indifference to any pain or pleasure, whether physical or mental, protected his calm mind. He was truly **vītarāgabhayakrodhaḥ**, i.e. free from attachment, fear, or anger.

He remained the same in his attitude towards his physical body. Complete detachment from earthly pain and pleasures kept him far away from the tribulations of normal life. At times, he was bestowed with so many expensive gifts by kings, wealthy men, and devotees. However, he never even touched them and distributed them to others in need.

During the cold winter season, many shawls and rugs were given to him as gifts so that he could be comfortable under the cold skies, but he remained in his naked state in complete tranquility.

Attraction to mundane pleasures begets sorrow and pain to normal humans, and thus one gets distracted from the pursuit of emancipation of the soul. Trailanga Swami was free from anger and envy, attraction or temptation for earthly pleasures. Thus he had always been a free soul yearning only to merge further into the Supreme Reality.

He had nothing mundane to lose or gain and that detachment was his inherent spiritual power. In stormy monsoon days, at times, he rescued many passengers of storm-struck boats that had capsized, fearlessly diving into the furious waves of the Ganges. He was a master over his own life because both life and death were no different to him.

It is not surprising that the truly wise people are free from anger. Anger usually originates from unfulfilled desires, and life frequently does not provide the opportunity to fulfill those desires. This condition generates despondence and eventually fury in the unsatisfied man.

Such a man's thoughts are mirrored on his face. In English it is opined that "Face is the index of mind"; or as the popular saying in India goes: "*Rogi, bhogi aur yogi—aankhse mishan aur aankh se pehchan*" (One can discern whether a person is a patient suffering from a disease, a hedonist or a sadhu, simply by looking at their eyes).

Though evolved saints can perceive a person's thoughts by just glancing at them due to their foresight, even a normal person can perceive the anger reflecting in the eyes and face of a man. Likewise, calm, even natured people's faces are, therefore, much more pleasant to look at. Sometimes anger can turn a man into a devil himself, and one can even become a killer very easily in a fit of anger.

Trailanga Swami was a completely free soul and no vice of any kind existed in him. It is indeed a pity that wicked and ignorant people tortured his divine body brutally at times, but he paid no heed to them at all and never became vindictive against any of them. He was immensely merciful to them and never even cursed them for their misbehaviour.

It would not be out of place to say here that in this modern world, people seem to be inclined to dishonor, oppress and ignore these saints in various ways. They may remain indifferent but the Almighty never forgives them for any sinful acts against great souls—God is never merciful to any such sort of arrogance and is always ruthless against such sinners.

यः सर्वत्रानभिस्नेहस्तत्तत्प्राप्य शुभाशुभम्।

नाभिनन्दति न द्वेष्टि तस्य प्रज्ञा प्रतिष्ठिता॥

yaḥ sarvatrānabhisnehastattatprāpya śubhāśubham |
nābhinandati na dveṣṭi tasya prajñā pratiṣṭhitā ||
(The Bhagavad Gita 2:57)

Translation: *One who is without attachment in every respect, neither rejoices nor curses obtaining correspondingly good or evil; he is established in perfect knowledge.*

It is said that love, caring attitude, affection etc. establish life properly on a solid foundation. People are happy to love and be loved, without love life becomes meaningless, and people might become emotionless and passionless. Given that, what is the actual message of God to man?

Does he like his creations to be emotionless? Not at all! However, our love is narrow and selfish, and does not usually extend to loving and caring for all. As the ancient hymn goes:

He prayeth well, who loveth well

Both man and bird and beast.

He prayeth best, who loveth best

All things both great and small.

For the dear God who loveth us,

He made and loveth all.

Excessive love directed at a narrow (selfish) cause breeds indifference to others, and takes us farther away from God. The holy Gita recommends that we show compassion to everyone and everything and become more selfless in our love. So the wise men merge themselves in the Supreme Consciousness and enjoy an eternal bond of love between man and God.

To avoid increasing attachment, Trailanga Swami asked his near devotees and disciples to go away far from him. In their days of suffering, they used to visit him and having been provided respite by the blissful Swami, they once again had to leave his place.

Trailanga Swami was apathetic to his own body, but he was deeply compassionate towards others. For his grace and blessings, a steady stream of suffering men would come to him and he was always compassionate towards them. Indeed, "*He prayed best*" because he loved the creations of the creator, as much as he loved the creator!

The average man classifies those things as 'good' that help him indulge his lust for material pleasures, and those as 'bad' that do not satisfy his material desires. However, a wise soul is above all such judgement, since his love for God is full of the deep devotion of one who perceives God as having manifested every where in nature—in men and women, in the green of the leaves, in the bright light of the sun, in the blowing breeze and everything else in the universe.

Likewise, the dark nights where there is reason for sorrow is also viewed as the manifestation of God's will, and therefore it is nothing to be agitated about. Actually, such a soul will not perceive anything to be worthier than the yearning for God, and will feel only intense love for God, the Lord of all creation. So, the honor from the King of Ujjain during the boat ride and the subsequent insults showered on him after a short while (when king's favourite sword was thrown by the Swamiji in the Ganges water) resulted in the same reaction from the Swamiji—*Indifference*.

यदा संहरते चायं कूर्मोऽङ्गानीव सर्वशः।

इन्द्रियाणीन्द्रियार्थेभ्यस्तस्य प्रज्ञा प्रतिष्ठिता॥

yadā saṁharate cāyaṁ kūrmo'gānīva sarvaśaḥ |
indriyāṇīndriyārthebhyastasya prajñā pratiṣṭhitā ||
(The Bhagavad Gita 2:58)

Translation: *When one completely withdraws the senses similarly as the tortoise withdraws its limbs from the objects of the senses, he is established in perfect knowledge.*

Just like a tortoise can withdraw its limbs back into its shell, similarly the sages can direct their sensory perception inwards, and with a still, content mind, their consciousness soars up high into the realms of the Infinite. External sense organs of man are actually controlled by an internal organ, mind.

Through these organs, man perceives everything in the external world. If one can control the mind enough to prevent distraction from sensory organs, achievement of true tranquility is possible.

The external world is always attractive and alluring to our sense organs, which are constantly stimulated by them, and herein lies the significance of withdrawing and redirecting the senses inwards. A tortoise gathers its limbs into its shell but does not render them useless; likewise, the spiritual aspirants also redirect those senses to reach higher and higher spiritual states. This becomes possible only because they can control any stimulation from their external sense organs.

Trailanga Swami had reached the Supreme Entity—reaching God Himself was his sole desire— and thus he was a free soul. *Bhakti* or devotion is nothing but selfless love for God and nothing other than God is worthy enough to be the essential objective of human life. Only our Creator, the Lord of the Universe, is worthy of this type of love, and if and when we feel His closeness to us, our life becomes meaningful and happy. We must follow this truth that was heard from the holy lips of Trailanga Swami.

Yukta Yogi Trailanga Swami

जितात्मनः प्रशान्तस्य परमात्मा समाहितः।

शीतोष्णसुखदुःखेषु तथा मानापमानयोः॥

jitātmanaḥ praśāntasya paramātmā samāhitaḥ |
śītoṣṇasukhaduḥkheṣu tathā mānāpamānayoḥ ||

(The Bhagavad Gita 6:7)

Translation: *The being who has conquered the mind, transcending the dualities of cold, heat, happiness, distress, honor and dishonor is firmly established with the Ultimate Consciousness within*

The men (soul) who haved triumphed over the desires for material and sensory pleasures and have acquired peace are independent, and always indifferent to temptation. Such a person is beyond the feelings of hot and cold, happiness and sorrows, honor or dishonor; and therefore is referred to as a '*Yukta Yogi*'.

An examination of Trailanga Swami's life tells us that he was beyond any of the abovementioned conditions prevalent in normal life. He dedicated his heart and soul to God and was indifferent to the scorching sun or to the biting cold or to fiery winds.

Trailanga Swami had also conquered hunger and thirst; based on his vow of non-seeking (*achayaka*), he never asked for food and whenever he felt like eating something, he was fed food by others, but he never took food with his own hands. Several times, there were periods of days at a stretch without any food consumption by him, and on some other occasions he ingested excessive quantities of food without any adverse result.

Shri Shri Shankari Mataji herself narrated that she herself had once fed her Guru 40 seers of food at a time!

ज्ञानविज्ञानतृप्तात्मा कूटस्थो विजितेन्द्रियः ।

युक्त इत्युच्यते योगि समलोष्टाश्मकाञ्चनः ॥

jñānaviñānatriptātmā kūṭastho vijitendriyaḥ |
yukta ityucyate yogi samaloṣṭrāśmakāñcanaḥ ||
(The Bhagavad Gita – 6:8)

Translation: *One perfected in the science of uniting the individual consciousness with the Ultimate Consciousness by acquired Vedic knowledge and direct realisation within the self, fixed in this state with senses fully controlled observing with equal vision a clot of dirt, a stone or gold is declared to be realised.*

Only that yogi, who posesses the wisdom in its true sense as mentioned in the *shastras* (scriptures) deserves the title of a '*Yukta Yogi*'. Such a one is detached from any earthly desires, and is indifferent to pleasure or pain. Such a one is a renunciate by heart. A piece of gold and a lump of clay are the same to them; they crave nothing because they posess the ultimate wealth—the grace of God. Everyone, whether they are monarchs or poor men, will salute such a person and bow down before their greatness. That is why the saying in Sanskrit that:

स्वदेशे पुज्यते राजा विद्वान् सर्वत्र पुज्यते

svadeśe pujyate rājā vidvān sarvatra pujyate

Translation: *A king is worshiped only in his own country, but a learned man is honored everywhere.*

Saints like Trailanga Swami are rare in this world. He had deep first-hand knowledge of the scriptures, and absorbed in the depths of spiritual pursuits, he had experienced most of it first-hand.

सुहृन्मित्रार्युदासिनमध्यस्थद्वेष्यबन्धुषु।

साधुष्वपि च पापेषु समबुद्धिविर्शिष्यते॥

suhrnmitrāryudāsinamadhyasthadveṣyabandhuṣu |
sādhuṣvapi ca pāpeṣu samabuddhivirśiṣyate ||

(The Bhagavad Gita 6:9)

Translation: *But more superior is the one who with spiritual intelligence acts equally towards natural well-wishers, affectionate well-wishers, enemies, those indifferent to disputes, mediators of disputes, the envious, friends, saintly person as well as the sinful.*

The person who is a *Yukta Yogi* exhibits detachment from everything—whether that is a friend or a foe, an honest or a dishonest person, a saint or an imposter. Such a person is superior in class to the man who has merely perceived no difference between Gold and clay. A *Yukta Yogi* never gets attached to anybody nor does he disdain anybody. He does not distinguish between a pious man and sinner, since he perceives them to be identical.

"A Jagate Keu Karo Shatru Mitra Noy I

Byabahare Shatru Mitra Parichay Hoy II"

Yogis and sadhus do not despise the sinner; they despise the sin. Trailanga Swami treated everybody consistently in a calm, placid, and pleasing manner.

Trailanga Swami—The Embodiment of God

चतुर्विधा भजन्ते मां जनाः सुकृतिनोऽर्जुन।

आर्तो जिज्ञासुरर्थार्थी ज्ञानी च भारतर्षभ॥

caturvidhā bhajante māṁ janāḥ sukṛtino'rjuna |
ārto jijñāsurarthārthī jñānī ca bhāratarṣabha ||
(The Bhagavad Gita 7:16)

Translation: *O best of the Bharatas, four types of pious persons render devotional service unto Me; the distressed, the seeker of knowledge, desirers of wealth, and men of wisdom*

There are four types of righteous people on earth who worship Shri Krishna:

1) **ārto** — Those who are distressed; i.e those who suffer from earthly ailments like diseases, mourning, poverty;

2) **jijñāsu** — Inquisitive, seekers of knowledge, those yearning to learn the Supreme Truth;

3) **arthārthī** — One who seeks money for earthly and spiritual purposes or for philanthropic activities;

4) **jñānī** — The wise, who are blessed with the knowledge of the Supreme Spirit, that '*Vasudeva Sarvam*'—God is Omniponent, yearning only to achieve the divine grace, worship me intently.

"*Sab devatakei pujan kori, Aapan ishtadev ke bhajan kori*" (Glossary 1) is their motto. Actually man's selfless devotion for God unites the Guru, the disciple and the Supreme Consciousness in an eternal bond. He exists in selfless love of the devotee when the devotee worships God with the intensity of a lover of unflinching faith. He feels his omnipresence, not perceiving Him only in the distant heavens.

तेषां ज्ञानी नित्ययुक्त एकभक्तिर्विशिष्यते।

प्रियो हि ज्ञानिनोऽत्यर्थमहं स च मम प्रियः॥

teṣāṁ jñānī nityayukta ekabhaktirviśiṣyate |
priyo hi jñānino'tyarthamahaṁ sa ca mama priyaḥ ||
(The Bhagavad Gita 7:17)

Translation: *Among them the man of wisdom always engaged exclusively in devotional service is superior; since to the cultivator of wisdom I am extremely dear and he is dear to Me.*

Of these four righteous classes of people, the fourth is the best because their love for God is always transcending, profound, and all engulfing. Thus they make Me come down to unite with these super souls as a lover of pure devotion.

उदाराः सवर एवैते ज्ञानि त्वात्मैव मे मतम्।

आस्थितः स हि युक्तात्मा मामेवानुत्तमां गतिम्॥

udārāḥ savara evaite jñāni tvātmaiva me matam |
āsthitaḥ sa hi yuktātmā māmevānuttamāṁ gatim ||
(The Bhagavad Gita 7:18)

Translation: *All these persons are certainly worthy; but in My opinion the man of wisdom is one with Me; because he is situated solely in self-realization of Me as the highest achievement.*

All these indicators of a truly self-realised person full of wisdom as indicated by Lord Krishna in the Bhagava Gita are evident in the life of Trailanga Swami.

अद्वेष्टा सर्वभूतानां मैत्रः करुण एव च।

निर्ममो निरहंकारः समदुःखसुखः क्षमी ॥

adveṣṭā sarvabhūtānāṁ maitraḥ karuṇa eva ca |
nirmamo nirahaṁkāraḥ samaduḥkhasukhaḥ kṣamī ||
(The Bhagavad Gita 12:13)

adveṣṭā sarvabhūtānāṁ — Non-envious towards all living entities — This attribute of the devotee who loves all of God's creations and who perceives God in all of His creations was evident in the holy life of Trailanga Swami. He never held any grudge against anyone, and in fact he was merciful to even those who tried to hurt him.

maitraḥ karuṇa eva ca — Benevolent & Compassionate — Trailanga Swami was the very epitome of compassion and he had a soul full of kindness, empathy, and affection for all beings. He never used the *siddhis* he clearly possessed for his own pleasures or comfort; but only used them out of spontaneous compassion and love for the distressed to solve their problems.

nirmamo — With no sense of proprietorship — A truly self-realized man is beyond any egoistic attitude and attitude of self-importance or a sense of ownership never exists within him. They understand and realize that conceit arises from ignorance. Trailanga Swami was clearly beyond such petty vanities.

nirahaṁkāraḥ — A truly realized man is always humble, modest and free of any vain pride. Such a person never considers himself as all powerful. The scriptures mention three types of pride:

Ahang sarbamidam biswam paramatmahchyutan

Manyasteeti sanbitya parama sajyamkriti

Sarbasmat byatiriktohahand balagradapyaham tanu

Iti ys sanbido Brahman dwitiyahat kriti shuva

Pani padadi matrohayamitreba nischayah

Ahankarastree yohasou loukikostacchu eba saha

The central Idea of the aforesaid versions from the *shastras*:

1) I am the monarch of all I survey, I am the omnipotent super soul, there is nothing but me—such tendency of thinking is the Supreme Pride.

2) I am abstracted from everything and finer than point of a single piece of hair—such thinking of a person places him in the second place—the better state of pride.

3) This part mortal body is 'me'— such is the thought of the lowest, the 3rd category of pride.

Trailanga Swami belonged to the mental state of '*Soham*' (I Am That) and this was manifested in his kind and merciful approach to all and sundry irrespective of any so called divisions or category of people. But his mental state was far above the lower concepts of common place people.

samaduḥkhasukhaḥ — Equal in distress or happiness — Trailanga Swami was completely indifferent and detached such that the environment like hot summers or cold winter, praise, or abuse from people had no impact on him. But he was compassionate enough at the same time to be sympathetic to people in agony or distress.

kṣamī — Tolerant, merciful — Trailanga Swami was all-merciful whose heart was filled with deep compassion. He was never angry, never displayed any malevolence to anyone, and was the living example of forgiveness.

सन्तुष्टः सततं योगी यतात्मा दृढनिश्चयः।

मय्यर्पितमनोबुद्धिर्यो मद्भक्तः स मे प्रियः ॥

santuṣṭaḥ satataṁ yogī yatātmā dṛḍhaniścayaḥ |
mayyarpitamanobuddhiryo madbhaktaḥ sa me priyaḥ ||
(The Bhagavad Gita 12:14)

Translation: *The always content one perfecting the science of uniting the individual consciousness with the Ultimate Consciousness, self-controlled, with unflinching determination, dedicating mind and spiritual intelligence upon Me is very dear to Me.*

The person who possesses determination, restraint, and is perfectly content in any state of life is especially dear to Me . Such a person who offers his never-failing loyalty and love to me becomes My favourite.

santuṣṭaḥ satataṁ — Always content — A person can always be content if he is — detached from mundane matters and only yearns for the grace of God. Trailanga Swami was merged into the Supreme Consciousness since his very early childhood days. So he never appeared to be despondent, and was unafflicted by any mundane, material desires.

yogī — The true devotees are single mindedly focused on spiritual pursuits.

yatātmā — Self-control — Sensual and material desires are the root cause behind all the restlessness in a man. The obstacles on the path to self-realization include ardent passions or desires of any kind, and Trailanga Swami had shielded himself with absolute control such that he wasn't bothered by any of these things at all.

dṛḍhaniścayaḥ — With unflinching determination — The singular and relentless pursuit of God kept him merged into his devotional activities although his long life.

mayyarpitamanobuddhiryo — Dedicating the mind and spiritual intelligence upon Me — The Swami was completely and solely dedicated only towards his spiritual *sadhana*, and nothing else at all

यस्मान्नोद्विजते लोको लोकान्नोद्विजते च यः।

हर्षामर्षभयोद्वेगैर्मुक्तो यः स च मे प्रियः॥

yasmānnodvijate loko lokānnodvijate ca yaḥ |

harṣāmarṣabhayodvegairmukto yaḥ sa ca me priyaḥ ||
(The Bhagavad Gita 12:15)

Translation: *One from whom any person is never disturbed and one who is never disturbed by any person and who is freed from the mundane pleasures, anger, fear, and anxiety, such a one is very dear to Me.*

yasmānnodvijate — One from whom no person is ever disturbed — The heart free of any anxiety, tensionless in any sphere or state of life, is an indicator of a noble soul. Trailanga Swami was completely in that state throughout his vast span of life. Here we feel it worthy to opine that the Supreme Consciousness—God—who manifested in the form of Lord Krishna is always approachable to sincere and pure-hearted devotees who can abstain from all the desires for material comforts and pleasures.The path to heaven is wide enough for devotees who have a pure heart, and this way to Divinity leads to the Kingdom of God, the meeting place, the confluence of saints. Trailanga Swami was accessible to any honest, pure, and loyal devotee.

lokānnodvijate — One who is never disturbed by any person — A devotee feels no anger nor malice even against people who are at times hurtful to him. He is always at peace and is tranquil in his divine soul, non-violent, merciful, loving. Even the normally ferocious animals like tigers, snakes change their character on getting close to such affectionate and merciful souls.

Dear readers! Imagine that amazing scene with your internal eye with vivid imagination—a fully grown large tiger, one who is a frightening predator, lying down at Trailanga Swami's feet as if it were his pet cat, and a trembling, dumb-founded Chief of Army to the Raja of Nepal standing observing the scene at a short distance.

Note: The Raja of Nepal was called as the Maharaj Adhiraj—the supreme monarch of Nepal.

harṣāmarṣabhayodvegairmukto — Free from mundane pleasures, anger, fear, and anxiety — Trailanga Swami's life and behaviour pretty much exemplifies this attribute. He was completely indifferent and detached at all times.

अनपेक्षः शुचिर्दक्ष उदासीनो गतव्यथः।

सर्वारम्भपरित्यागी यो मद्भक्तः स मे प्रियः॥

anapekṣaḥ śucirdakṣa udāsīno gatavyathaḥ |
sarvārambhaparityāgī yo madbhaktaḥ sa me priyaḥ ||
(The Bhagavad Gita 12:16)

Translation: *That devotee of Mine who is desireless, pure, expert, free from worry, free from agitation, unconcerned with any mundane endeavour; such a one is very dear to Me.*

anapekṣaḥ — Desireless — Trailanga Swami had completely surrended to the will of the Almighty, and as such did not have any mundane desires whatsoever.

śuci — Pure — No impurity could even reach him throughout the long journey of Swamiji's life.

dakṣa — Dependent on their desires, taste etc. people are oftenly confused to ascertain their 'dos' and 'don'ts', good or evil. Trailanga Swami depended only on the graceful Almighty and as such he was free of any such mental undulations. He remained ever-composed and firm.

udāsīno — True and sincere devotees are always detached from the trials and tribulations of life. They even do not pay any attention to such worries of mundane existence. Trailanga Swami's firm devotion to God was like the immovable polar star that always exists and is always steady in any state of existence.

gatavyathaḥ — Trailanga Swami was quite aloof from the pleasure and pains of life. There are many many examples that can be cited from the indidents of his holy life.

sarvārambhaparityāgī — Swamiji used to pursue his spiritual activities or any other external activities in the light of his knowledge of the Truth. He never felt egoistic while performing anything. Total submission to God was the underpinning of his spiritual pursuits. Shri Ramakrishna Paramhansa used to opine that the Holy Lord Vishweshwar has Himself incarnated in the mortal body of Trailanga Swami. Furthermore, the will of Lord Vishweshwar manifested via the medium of Trailanga Swami.

The Lord Vishweshwar graced so many fortunate men and women through the holy form of Trailanga Swami, thereby sowing the seeds for future spiritually elevated souls to keep the fires of *Sanatana Dharma* burning.

Bhaktiyoga

Shrimad Bhagavad Gita states:

यो न हृष्यति न द्वेष्टि न शोचति न काङ्क्षति।

शुभाशुभपरित्यागी भक्तिमान् यः स मे प्रियः ॥

yo na hṛṣyati na dveṣṭi na śocati na kāḍkṣati |
śubhāśubhaparityāgī bhaktimān yaḥ sa me priyaḥ ||

समः शत्रौ च मित्रे च तथा मानापमानयोः।

शीतोष्णसुखदुःखेषु समः संगविवर्जितः ॥

samaḥ śatrau ca mitre ca tathā mānāpamānayoḥ |
śītoṣṇasukhaduḥkheṣu samaḥ saṁgavivarjitaḥ ||

तुल्यनिन्दास्तुतिमौनी सन्तुष्टो येन केनचित्।

अनिकेतः स्थिरमतिर्भक्तिमान्मे प्रियो नरः ॥

tulyanindāstutimaunī santuṣṭo yena kenacit |
aniketaḥ sthiramatirbhaktimānme priyo naraḥ ||

(The Bhagavad Gita 12:17-19)

Translation:

One who rejoices not, dislikes not, grieves not, and desires not, impartial to both what is auspicious and inauspicious, engaged in devotional service; such a one is very dear to Me.

That person who is equal to an enemy as well as a friend, also in honor or dishonor, impartial in cold, heat, happiness and distress, exempt from attachment, equipoised in praise or repute, contemplating before speaking, satisfied with whatever comes on its own accord, not attached to domestic life, fixed in determination and engaged in devotional service; such a one is very dear to Me.

Truly spiritual souls perceive Lord Shiva, the Destroyer and Lord Vishnu, the Preserver in each and every mortal being. Such people are true and wholeheartedly servile to God. Such a saint is emancipated and exempt from any future birth.

The characteristics evident in Trailanga Swami, which as per the Gita are the hallmarks of a truly realised person, is completely corroborated by the hallmark of an emancipated saint according to the Upanishads, as quoted below:

मौनवान् निरहम्भावो निर्मानो मुक्तमत्सरः।

यः करोति गतोद्वेगः स जीवन्मुक्त उच्यते॥

maunavān nirahambhāvo nirmāno muktamatsaraḥ |
yaḥ karoti gatodvegaḥ sa jīvanmukta ucyate ||

(Mahopanishad 2:50)

Translation: *He who maintains silence, is free from ego, free from pride, does not envy any one, performs actions without any mental agitation, such a person is called a Jeevanmukta.*

We do not have to mention the characteristics as described in the *shlokas* in the holy Bhagavad Gita completely corroborate the hallmarks of a truly wise and well accomplished person (*Yukta Yogi*) as they have already been discussed previously. Some other symptoms relevant to his context are herewith mentioned below according to the ideology of *Satsanga*:

maunavān — Trailanga Swami practiced *mouna* (being silent) regularly, except on the night when he used to advise and preach to the dear ones and the disciples. We know the Bengali great sage Mahatma Vijaykrishna Goswami received his primary spiritual instructions from Trailanga Swami in Kashi when Swamiji broke his silence.

Talkative people are restless in their minds, and so it is important to observe the practice of silence so that one can focus properly on spiritual austeries. Of late, it is commonplace to see sadhus talking and preaching incessantly in front of large assemblies of people. But Trailanga Swami was far above providing spirituality based entertainment to the masses or trying to become popular as he was aloof and independent in his heart. He showered his grace on the common masses even while maintaining his vow of silence.

aniket — Trailanga Swami had never established any permanent dwelling or ashram . He was at home anywhere. We like to clarify the popular misconception regarding his existence during the last years of his life in Kashi being the very *math* or abbotage, is completely incorrect.

Trailanga Swami never accepted any sort of bondage in his long life. The *math* popularly known as the Trailanga Swami Math in Kashi is actually a house owned by Mangal Bhattji and family. The great sage became quite pleased with them, thanks to their sincere service rendered unto him when he was in sojourn at the Pancha Ganga Ghat on the banks of the Ganga, near Benimdhab Joradhwaja (pair of masts).

The compassionate Mahayogeshwar also agreed to stay in the open court yard of their house to work out his divine activities, responding to their sincere and heartfelt invitation. We have already mentioned that all of them served him with sincere and respectful care till his departure. Pure, devout, and servile to their Guru, the members of Mangal Bhattji's family were not at all financially affluent or rich; however they were rich in their devout hearts. So just to grace those devotees with his presence, '*Aniket*' (without any permanent address or dwelling) Trailanga Swamiji stayed there. He explicitly forbade any of his other disciples from staying at that place.

The Emancipated Soul— The Holy Trailanga Swami

One is obviously an emancipated soul when one realises that "*Yatra Jiva, Tatra Shiva*" (The Lord Shiva exists in all living beings), and understands the true significance of the term '*Shiva-Tattva*' (Becoming like the Lord Shiva) in his lifetime in the mortal world. Emancipation (*Jeevan Mukti*) is the greatest degree of freedom, independence.

All the characteristics of an ideal devotee as per the holy Bhagavad Gita were clearly evident in the life of Trailanga Swami.

Likewise, all the hallmarks of an emancipated soul, as described in the Upanishads, were also clearly visible in the holy life of Trailanga Swami. If one reads the following *shlokas* carefully and contemplates over them, one can realize that the hallmarks of a truly emancipated soul are described identically in both the holy Bhagavad Gita and the Upanishads.

मौनवान् निरहम्भावो निर्मानो मुक्तमत्सरः।

यः करोति गतोद्वेगः स जीवन्मुक्त उच्यते॥ १॥

maunavān nirahambhāvo nirmāno muktamatsaraḥ |
yaḥ karoti gatodvegaḥ sa jīvanmukta ucyate || 1 ||

सर्वत्र विगतस्नेहो यः साक्षिवदवस्थितः।

निरिच्छे वर्तते कार्ये स जीवन्मुक्त उच्यते॥ २॥

sarvatra vigatasneho yaḥ sākṣivadavasthitaḥ |
niricche vartate kārye sa jīvanmukta ucyate || 2 ||

येन धर्ममधर्मं च मनोमननमीहितम्।

सर्वमन्तः परित्यक्तं स जीवन्मुक्त उच्यते॥ ३॥

yena dharmamadharma ca manomananamīhitam |
sarvamantaḥ parityaktaṁ sa jīvanmukta ucyate || 3 ||

आपतत्सु यथाकालं सुखदुःखेष्वनारतः।

न हृष्यति ग्लायति यः स जीवन्मुक्त उच्यते॥ ४॥

āpatatsu yathākālaṁ sukhaduḥkheṣvanārataḥ |
na hṛṣyati glāyati yaḥ sa jīvanmukta ucyate || 4 ||

हर्षामर्षभयक्रोधकामकार्पण्यदृष्टिभिः।

न परामृश्यते योऽन्तः स जीवन्मुक्त उच्यते॥ ५॥

harṣāmarṣabhayakrodhakāmakārpaṇyadṛṣṭibhiḥ |
na parāmṛśyate yo'ntaḥ sa jīvanmukta ucyate || 5 ||

इप्सितानीप्सिते न स्तो यस्यान्तर्वर्तिदृष्टिषु।

सुषुप्तिवध्यश्चरति स जीवन्मुक्त उच्यते॥ ६॥

ipsitānīipsite na sto yasyāntarvartidṛṣṭiṣu |
suṣuptivadhyaścarati sa jīvanmukta ucyate || 6 ||

अध्यात्मरतिरासीनः पूर्णः पावनमानसः।

प्राप्तानुत्तमविश्रान्तिर्न किंचिदिह वाञ्चति।

यो जीवति गतस्नेहः वा स जीवन्मुक्त उच्यते॥ ७॥

adhyātmaratirāsīnaḥ pūrṇaḥ pāvanamānasaḥ |
prāptānuttamaviśrāntirna kiṁcidiha vājhcati |

yo jīvati gatasnehaḥ vā sa jīvanmukta ucyate || 7 ||

रागद्वेषौ सुखं दुःखं धर्माधर्मौ फलाफले।

यः करोत्यनपेक्ष्यैव स जीवन्मुक्त उच्यते॥ ८॥

rāgadveṣau sukhaṁ duḥkhaṁ dharmādharmau phalāphale |
yaḥ karotyanapekṣyaiva sa jīvanmukta ucyate || 8 ||

कट्वम्ललवणं तिक्तममृष्टं मृष्टमेव च।

सममेव च यो भुङ्क्ते स जीवन्मुक्त उच्यते॥ ९॥

kaṭvamlalavaṇaṁ tiktamamṛṣṭaṁ mṛṣṭameva ca |
samameva ca yo bhuṛkte sa jīvanmukta ucyate || 9 ||

जरामरणमापच्च राज्यं दारिद्रयमेव च।

रम्यमित्येव यो भुङ्क्ते स जीवन्मुक्त उच्यते॥ १०॥

jarāmaraṇamāpacca rājyaṁ dāridrayameva ca |
ramyamityeva yo bhuṛkte sa jīvanmukta ucyate || 10 ||

उद्वेगानन्दरहितः समया स्वच्छया धिया।

न शोचते न चोदेति स जीवन्मुक्त उच्यते॥ ११॥

udvegānandarahitaḥ samayā svacchayā dhiyā |
na śocate na codeti sa jīvanmukta ucyate || 11 ||

जन्मस्थितिविनाशेषु सोदयास्तमयेषु च।

सममेव मनो यस्य स जीवन्मुक्त उच्यते॥ १२॥

janmasthitivināśeṣu sodayāstamayeṣu ca |
samameva mano yasya sa jīvanmukta ucyate || 12 ||

न किंचन द्वेष्टि तथा न किंचिदपि काङ्क्षति।

भुङ्क्ते यः प्रकृतान्भोगान्स जीवन्मुक्त उच्यते॥ १३॥

na kiṁcana dveṣṭi tathā na kiṁcidapi kāḍkṣati |
bhuḍkte yaḥ prakṛtānbhogānsa jīvanmukta ucyate || 13 ||

शान्तसंसारकलनः कलावानपि निष्कलः।

यः सचित्तोऽपि निश्चित्तः स जीवन्मुक्त उच्यते॥ १४॥

śāntasaṁsārakalanaḥ kalāvānapi niṣkalaḥ |
yaḥ sacitto'pi niścittaḥ sa jīvanmukta ucyate || 14 ||

यः समस्तार्थजालेषु व्यवहार्यपि निःस्पृहः।

परार्थेष्विव पूर्णात्मा स जीवन्मुक्त उच्यते॥ १५॥

yaḥ samastārthajāleṣu vyvahāryapi niḥspṛhaḥ |
parāretheṣviva pūrṇātmā sa jīvanmukta ucyate || 15 ||

॥ ॐ तत् सत्॥

|| om tat sat ||

Chapter 10. Lord Vishweshwar and Trailanga Swami

Shri Ramakrishna Paramhamsa of Bengal used to frequently say: "I saw that Lord Vishweshwar (Shiva) Himself had manifested in the mortal body of Trailanga Swami. His presence makes the entire holy city of Kashi dazzle with divine brightness."

(Leela Prasanga—Swami Saradananda)

A human being can attain godliness by achieving divine abilities by dint of spiritual austerities—this is not an exaggeration at all. It is an accepted and universally acknowledged truth.

God is the Creator of the universe. He is Omnipotent. He is propitious, Absolute, perpetually pure, and Omniscient. As part of the divine play, He went from one to many—converted himself in multiple forms and with multiple names, even though there is only One everywhere —"*Eko'ham Bahusyam*".

He revealed Himself to metaphysically ignorant beings, who were His own creations. These ignorant beings were oblivious of their own innate God and perceived Him as a completely separate entity, a great power different from them. They can not think of themselves as anything other than creature-like statues around 5 feet tall, a negligible and merely insignificant entity in the context of the vast universe, controlled by place, time, and objects. But they have immense possibilities themselves, to attain the supreme wisdom or super consciousness, and to realise the creator-destructor-preserver omnipotent entity innately present within their bodies, and thus achieve absolute peace, satisfaction, and limitless pleasure.

सर्वभूतेषु यः पश्येद्भगवद्भावमात्मनः।

भूतानि भगवति आत्मन्येष भागवतोत्तमः॥

sarvabhūteṣu yaḥ paśyedbhagavadbhāvamātmanaḥ |
bhūtāni bhagavati ātmanyeṣa bhāgavatottamaḥ ||
(Shrimad Bhagavatam 11:2:45)

The person who can see God in all the beings, and see all beings in God, is the best devotee.

They can develop the internal godliness within themselves, and thus realize the Supreme Truth—God. The Ordainer of the universe benevolently provided ways in the laws governing His vast universe such that even the ignorant beings could slowly make spiritual progress, day by day.

The divine power, knowledge, love and pleasure, that are immanent in embodied souls since ages, get fully manifested in saints by dint of their spiritual austerities. These qualities and riches of the Divine bloom in them fully and the desires of God are then revealed in these beings that attain divine success and grace.

Such advanced sages that possess immense spiritual riches ultimately unite with their Creator; however, in the meanwhile these blessed souls exist in the material world as the living epitome of God.

Thus, the omnipresent God reveals Himself as these saints in their mortal forms, and in that manner, the Lord enjoys his ownself via his own creations, *Eko'ham Bahusyam*—The absolute God becomes many and bestows his own creation with success.

Trailanga Swamiji had gained immense spiritual riches like knowledge of Truth, and characteristics like compassion and love for all beings were evident in him. He had attained divinity while existing in his physical body, and lived in this material world with the great feelings of oneness with his Creator. He was the living example of the extreme meaning behind God's creation. All the wisdom, kindness, auspiciousness of the Supreme Entity were manifested in his holy self and he had become free of any ego or vanity. This was the real '*Soham*' (I am That). The opinion of Shri Ramakrishna Paramhamsa that "The Holy Lord Vishweshwara and the holy Trailanga Swami are one and the same" was completely true. Just like only a diamond can cut a diamond, likewise only a truly God-realized saint can identify and recognise another God-realised saint.

॥ ॐ तत् सत् ॥

|| om tat sat ||

Chapter 11. Mother Ganga and Trailanga Swami

Maa Ganga, or the holy river Ganga, has a special importance in the long life of Trailanga Swami. Readers would recall that Swamiji lived around 100 years of his much longer life on its holy banks in Varanasi. A great part of his sojourn in Varanasi was spent in and around the waters of the Ganga. Frequently he used to remain submerged under the Ganges waters, and quite often he would be floating on its surface. Nobody other than Swamiji was known to have stayed submerged in the waters of the river. The residents of the holy Kashidham would quite often become dumbstruck watching the holy sage deeply absorbed in his meditation and in that state floating around along with the currents of the river.

For his long association and divine play in the lap of the mother Ganga, the holy river, people worshiped Trailanga Swami as *Ganga Nandan*—son of the mother Ganges.

Readers might recall that we have alluded to Trailanga Swami as Bhishmadev in the *shlokas* in the preface titled "Shri Shri Trailangashtakam Stotra".

Trailanga Swami also remained a life-long celibate, just like Bhishmadev, and underwent intense austerities as a *brahmachari* throughout his long holy life. The Bhismadev of *Dwapara Yuga* had abdicated his royal inheritance for the benefit of his younger brother, and likewise our venerable Trailanga Swami—the Bhismadev of Kali Yuga—had sacrificed his paternal wealth for the benefit of his younger brother.

These are not ordinary events in the life of regular people, but rather, in the religious history of India, these are watershed events that will remain perpetually significant and noteworthy.

He renounced the world leaving behind the immense wealth inherited by him from his father and became a renunciate. The single-minded dedication to truth, and the strength of character that was so evident in

Bhishmadev's life was also equally evident in the life of Trailanga Swamij. Trailanga Swami voluntarily left his physical body on his own birthday, and so did Bhishmadev as well.

Birth and death are subject to divine principles and not something that can be controlled by humans. Therefore these instances from the life of Bhishmadev and Trailanga Swami were remarkable exceptions.

The divinity within the saints is usually evident while they are living in the physical body, and so it is indeed not surprising if even the eventual exit from their physical bodies also has some super natural characteristics, in some way!! Trailanga Swamiji notified his disciples almost a month in advance about the date of his *Mahasamadhi.*

Likewise, Bhishmadev also stayed on the bed of arrows in the war field of Kurukshetra, awaiting the appropriate moment to pass away, from when it was the winter solstice (From about 22nd June to 21st December) until the advent of the summer solstice.

Maharaja Yudishthira and his other companions got immensely valuable spiritual advice (most notably the Vishnu Sahasranama) from the great Bhishmadev while he was lying on the bed of arrows.

The news of Trailanga Swami's anticipated *samadhi* was also circulated about one month in advance; and during that period of time a large number of his disciples, devotees, sages, *paramhansas,* and general public visited him to pay their respects, and to receive invaluable spiritual advice. On the date previously announced, Swamiji exited his physical body through *Agni Yoga*.

It almost felt like a reprisal of the *Shanti Parva* section of the Mahabharata, which narrates the incidents of the great Bhishmadev's last stage of life while lying on the bed of arrows, comforting, satisfying listeners with his valuable advice. From time immemorial, these stories form the fabric of Indian culture and history, and would continue to do so in the future as well.

Note: We further like to suggest that it is for this reason that the *Chiranjivis* (immortals), who are beyond death and are present across the time span indicated by the four *yugas*, exist—in other words, they are the immortal witnesses who are responsible for preserving *Sanatana Dharma*.

"Ashwathama Balir Vyaasoh Hanumashcha Vibheeshana I
Kripaacharya cha Parashuramam Saptaita Chiranjeevanam II"

The perpetual memory of the Seven *Rishis* exists till date in the holy Puri-dham. In addition we would like to say that such holy memories are imprinted in the countless hearts of the Indians, and so how can Hinduism ever perish? The eternal Absolute Truth Itself is the perpetual religion *Sanatana Dharama*—it can never be extinct.

We hope in the context of the relation between Trailanga Swami and Mother Ganga, a few details about the river *Maa* Ganga will not be irrelevant.

For all the Hindus, especially the dwellers on its banks, taking holy dips into the Ganga daily without fail is a recommended practice. Likewise, drinking of the Ganges water is also recommended. The qualities of the water of this river had been detailed in the scriptures of the Hindu *shastras* in many ways. The literature of our country also describes this river as the holiest and enthroned Maa Ganga at the altar of the Supreme.

पुश्पेशु जाती पुरुशेशु विष्णुः

नारीशु रम्भा नगरीशु कान्ची

नदीशु गन्गा च नृप्शु रामः

puśpeśu jātī puruśeśu viṣṇuḥ
nārīśu rambhā nagarīśu kāncī
nadīśu gangā ca nrpśu rāmaḥ

Translation: *The best among flowers is the Jasmine, among beings it is Vishnu, among women it is Rambha, among towns it is Kanchi, among rivers it is the Ganges, and among Princes it is Rama.*

To the Hindus, the waters of the Ganges are considered as the holiest, providing sancitity to the body and the mind.

Ganges water is a must-have element in India for *pujas* (worship rituals) and offerings made to the deities. Not just the Hindus, even Muslim kings and people following the Muslim faith in this country have cherished the water of the Ganga for its purity, as well as treating it as divine. Even the British, during their two hundred years stay in India, profusely praised this holy river.

The length of Mother Ganges (the river) is about 1,600 miles. On the banks of this holy river the Aryan Civilisation was born; and it blossomed and built a solid foundation influencing the life, culture, values, and religion and thus became the integral part of our life. In this age as well, the excellent socio-economic progress of the north-eastern part of India can be viewed as the blessings of the river.

Emanating from the glaciers of Gangotri in the Himalayas, it crosses the Shivalika Ganges near Haridwar into the plains. It flows continuously from the north towards the southern part of India.

In its course of flow it gradually crosses places like Yukta Pradesh, Kanpur, Prayag (Allahabad), Vindhyachal, the holy city of Varanasi, Ghazipur, Balia, Patna etc. and then enters West Bengal at Triveni in Hooghly district in the name of Mukta Triveni. Then it flows down through the inlet Sagar Sangam or Gangasagar and finally merges into the confluence of the ever-lasting Bay of Bengal. Here at the confluence, the river and the sea become one and inseparable.

Ceaseless are the rivers that originate from the vast blue oceans or seas. Water from the surface of the seas evaporates due to the rays of the sun, and goes high up in the blue sky and then condenses in clouds. These mass of clouds eventually turn into rainfall. Rain water falling on the mountains condenses into silvery snow slabs and glaciers.

In summer, these glaciers melt and flow downward as rivers with different names and courses, and finally after long journeys they again join the seas—their origin. Seas seem to have a shape, but actually the sea water itself does not have any form or particular shape. It comes across as blue in color, in reality it is actually crystal clear and transluscent.

The men of wisdom tell us that due to its fathomless depth and the reflection of the blue sky above, the waters of oceans and seas look bluish!! Water takes the shape of its container, but when the container breaks down, water returns to its original form, having been mixed with the main source. One can not differentiate or trace out the Ganga, the Jamuna, or the Brahmaputra, in particular after they merge into the seas. The vapour particles are formless, but snow is visible in many forms. These facts are indisputable and scientifically proven.

The bubbles and waves that originate from the sea water ultimately dissolve in their origin. Likewise, life of the common man is mortal and finite, but great lives are eternal like the endless seas.

Let us evaluate the life of a man in the form of 'air'. Does it exist only in the body of man? Or only in the heart? No—life is omnipresent. It exists in the sky, air, the dazzling sun, blazing flame of fire, and into water, on the land (earth), and in the endless sky.

The muddy white waters of the Ganga and the bluish water of the river Jamuna can be seen differently here in the Prayag-dham. The reverse flow of the Ganga reaches the holy '*Shivpuri*' (Dwelling place of lord Shiva) Kashi-dham, from Prayag.

Books like "Kashi Mahatmya" provide a wonderful explanation of the reverse flow of Ganga from the down-plain lands to the upper area like Kashi-dham, which is geographically rare. People from India and abroad come here to enjoy boating on the waves of the Ganga near Kashi-dham. The Ganga near Kashi-dham is also referred to as '*Gyaan Ganga*' that flows northwards. It is said that one who passes away here in Kashi gets emancipated at once owing to the holiness and divinity of the place.

The man who breathes his last in the holy Kashi-dham is really fortunate as he gets the ever-merciful Lord Shiva's grace, who Himself utters the great *mantra* "Tarak Brahma Naam" in his ears:

हरे रामा हरे रामा रामा रामा हरे हरे।

हरे कृष्णा हरे कृष्णा कृष्णा कृष्णा हरे हरे॥

hare rāmā hare rāmā rāmā rāmā hare hare |
hare kṛṣṇā hare kṛṣṇā kṛṣṇā kṛṣṇā hare hare ||

And thus the dying man gets emanicipation. As someone taking refuge at the feet of the ever merciful Lord Shiva, he is bestowed with freedom from rebirth during his final journey leaving the mortal body!!

What a wonderful custom it is that is prevalent in the city of Kashi-dham! To honor the deceased person's soul, everybody pays tribute to the departed soul treating the physical body of the dead man as the seat of Lord Shiva Himself, while carrying the body to the burning *ghat* for cremation. While carrying the body thus, they also chant in unison, the perpetual truth "Shri Ram Naam Satya Hai". One can be successful in one's lifetime if one realises this truth while living this ephemeral life!!

Over the ages, countless *rishis*, *munis*, saints and sages have reached the zenith of spiritual success by performing their intense spiritual austerities sitting on the soil of the wide banks of the holy river. Even now there are many who perform spiritual activities of various types on those banks.

A few will chant silently using the beads of a rosary, and mutter inaudible repetitions of their prayers from the scriptures or the name of deities, others offer *pujas* and perform such other devotional activities regularly. Though their numbers have declined in the present age, yet the never-dying spirit of devotion is visible there. Besides this, the various festivities that happen on its banks have become world famous, and for this reason, generally the density of population is very high in the towns on the banks of this river.

The magnanimous descent of the Ganges from the heavens is an oft-repeated, favourite story of many. The tale narrates the sancitity of the banks of the river, and about the five gross elements—earth, water, fire, wind, ether and their graceful magnanimity, the grace of five deities i.e. Lord Shiva, Ganesh, Sun, Narayana, Mother Earth and their subtle significance, and the magnanimity of the slogan "*Badri Vishal Ki Jai*".

These stories narrated by the wise sages are comprehensible only to the one possessing enough subtle intelligence and perception. It is unfortunate indeed that due to the lack of *Brahmacharya* and the pursuit of sensory gratification many in this present age can not engage their subtle perceptions at all.

The land on which great saints like Bhishmadev and Trailanga Swami lived their holy lives and accomplished many things (usually regarded as impractical) by virtue of their perception of *Shukra Brahma* knowledge, has unfortunately become a place where not many attempt to venture down that path.

The living world is based on the *sukha shukra* (spermatozoa, in semen). It is endless, it is the power of potency; this potency is in the molecules of sperm, the reproductive cell that causes generations of human life to happen. But excessive discharge of semen expedites death. Real teachers are the ones who teach their students what is always necessary, and are those who can teach how one can attain immortality.

यद् यदाचरति श्रेष्ठस्तत्तदेवेतरो जनः।

स यत्प्रमाणं कुरुते लोकस्तदनुवर्तते॥

yad yadācarati śreṣṭhastattadevetaro janaḥ |
sa yatpramāṇaṁ kurute lokastadanuvartate ||

(The Bhagavad Gita 3:21)

Translation: *Whichever and however a great personality conducts himself, common men do also; whatever he accepts as authority that and that alone certainly the entire world will follow.*

We have already described the sanctity of the Ganges. To further quench the thirst of our inquisitive readers, let us narrate a few more stories:–

अश्वत्थः सर्ववृक्षाणां देवर्षीणां च नारद।

गन्धर्वाणां चित्ररथः सिद्धानां कपिलो मुनिः ॥

aśvatthaḥ sarvavṛkṣāṇāṁ devarṣīṇāṁ ca nārada |
gandharvāṇāṁ citrarathaḥ siddhānāṁ kapilo muniḥ ||

(The Bhagavad Gita 10:26)

Translation: *Of all the trees, I am the sacred banyan tree; of the divine sages, Narada Muni; of the Gandharvas, Chitraratha; and of perfected beings, I am Kapiladeva.*

In the ancient past, King Sagar, belonging to the lineage of the Surya dynasty (*Suryavamsa*) had 60,000 sons. These sons were destroyed to ashes by the curse of Kapila, the great *Muni*.

Kapila Muni suggested to Bhagiratha, who was a descendant of King Sagar, that he do penance to bring down the Ganga with her forms of *Tridhara* i.e. *Mandakini Ganga* in the heaven, *Bhogavati Ganga* in the nether region, and *Bhagirathi Ganga* on the earth.

Bhagirath did intense penance and succeeded in getting Ganga to descend from the heavens and thereby revive King Sagar's descendants. The blessings of the mother Ganga redeemed the Sagar dynasty, and Bhagiratha became immortal as a result of the noble deed. This story of Bhagirath and Mother Ganga is inscribed in our scriptures since ages. Another tale describes how the great sage Jahnu Muni, with his tremendous spiritual powers, drank the entire volume of the Ganga–water taking it in his palm as *aposhanam*, and then again discharged its entire flow through his knee secretly. Because of that, another name for Mother Ganga has become famous as '*Jahnavi*'.

We would like to emphasise further on the uniqueness of the Ganga that not only is this river recognized as the holiest , but in fact, its water is invigorating almost like it is the very nectar of the earth. Hopefully, this long discussion on this topic will not bore the dear readers, and hopefully they will be pleased to learn many wonderful details related to this great river.

Many of our respected readers are aware of the fact that ships traveling between India and Europe had to sail for months. Even the voyages through the "Cape of Good Hope" used to take at least 6 months. Afterwards voyages through the conduits of Arabian Seas and then through Suez Canal took at least one month. Suffice to say that it was a different era from this age of aeroplanes.

In those days the ships sailing from Calcutta port towards England used to carry the water of the Ganges in their reservoirs! The shipped water remained potable despite months of storage without any symptoms of impurities. In comparison, water taken and stored from other European countries used to become contaminated and impure during their voyage to India.

Struck by this purity of the Ganga water, scientists took an active interest and investigated the reason behind this purity. A gentleman named Mr. Hankin conducted experiments with the water from the Ganges in his laboratory in Agra and verified the amazing power of its invigorating nature and ability to remain pure.

From then on, the purity of Ganga-water was widely acknowledged by the British people. If properly stored in any clean vessel for up to 6 hours, the water remains potable.

Nevertheless, it is always recommended to boil the water before consumption. It will be recommended that for much better water purification, use of the flower called '*Nirmalee*' be made. The flower is available in the holy Kashi-dham and some other adjacent areas.

One is supposed to rub the flower at the mouth of the vessel containing the water; after which one is usually astonished to notice that even the sediments of turbid waters vanish, due to the flower's excellent purifying strength.

Use of the flower '*Nirmalee*' leaves the water crystal clear and transparent. One will appreciate the medicinal properties of the holy Ganga water if one uses the flower; however, ignorant people do not believe it. In the same manner as the flower, we would like to opine here that the *Mahamantra* is as useful and powerful for the attainment of spiritual sanctity.

Any work executed with ardent devotion towards God and with a sincere heart must beget success, and will eventually result in tranquility of mind and soul. If we try hard enough, we can overcome the negative conditioning (*samskaras*) accumulated throughout successive births, with the help of prayers and *mantras* provided by saints and other divinely realised entities.

Our mind and soul will then become like a mirror, reflecting the divine image of God, the Supreme Creator. This is just like how one can see the water of the Ganges in the holy area of Haridwar shimmering and translucent during the summer, as in that time of the year there are no major currents in the river. Indeed, one can watch the fishes swimming playfully, and even the bottom of the river bed is clearly visible during summer in Haridwar.

The celebrated American novelist and astute writer Mark Twain visited India under his real name "Mr. Clemens" (Mark Twain was his pen name). He investigated the purity of the Ganga water and wrote in his book:–

"*The Indians regard and worship the water of the river Ganges for its purity since ages. It was unjust on the part of the Europeans and other country men of other religious who laughed at them for their belief in its sanctity.*"

It is unfortunate that when one cannot depend upon one's own knowledge, nothing but senseless judgment comes forth. People in the West often make fun of our religious faith saying it is based on the proclamations from sages, oracles, and the heavenly bodies. To be clear, it is not an offensive act per se, but we can demonstrate with concrete examples the wisdom and the knowledge of the present, past, and future that our ancestors and the *rishis* and sages posessed.

How did the *rishis* and *munis* discover the sanctifying power of the Ganges water, especially in those ancient ages? Were there bacteriologists present in India at that time? It is crystal clear that even before the time that the uncivilised races in both the oriental and occidental countries crossed the demarcation line from uncivilization to civilization, there were *rishis* and *munis* in India who existed with the pure knowledge of Truth and God.

They had gone beyond the mundane knowledge realms even since the advent of knowledge in to human consciousness happened. They ignored mundane, material wisdom and were happy and content with their riches of spiritual knowledge. Science, arts and any other branch of knowledge is achieveable only when intelligence and true conscience propels our inquisition towards the omniscient God.

Dedication to God is the only path that will help reach the absolute knowleldge. Misguided scientists, therefore, can not acquire any such wisdom. When the mind is calm and quiet and completely at rest, it is called as 'soul'; on the other hand a restless mind is a 'being', an ephemeral entity. Therefore, is it impossible for any intensely dedicated devotee to acquire true knowledge when devotion to God is the only cause?

The scriptures opine "*Jatra Jiv, Tatra Shiv*". This is the one aspect where Hinduism differs from the other religions. For last eighteen years on a daily basis we have been blessed listening to the spiritual advice given by the holy Trailanga Swami to our venerable Shri Shri Shankari Mataji, from her own mouth:–

"Maa, just realise the fact that God is the only true constant and eternal; and He is worshiped in different ways according to the difference of countries, angle of vision. People will do their work and will continue doing them according to their beliefs i.e. construction and erection of temples, churches, mosques etc. But how many of them realise that the Supreme Soul is beyond any earthly debate and confusion?"

"*Sarvam Khalvidam Brahma*"—Brahman, the Supreme Reality, is omnipotent and is beyond any cause and effect. Truely wise great men do not feel any difference of time, space, and object.

Could people of different religions and opinions draw any line of demarkation for 'Maa' or 'The Sky? *Mati* or the motherly soil and the sky remain the same anywhere, any time, and perpetually so. Likewise God Shri Hari Janardan is One, He receives various ideas, concepts. The five material elements appear to be true within our limited perception but there is also the invisible Truth only perceptible to the truly wise. Those wise men who can realise the Supreme Truth are venerable for the world without any debate. Truth is beyond any debate or any confusion, and Truth is beyond any language or image.

For the awareness of people stupified by the occidental civilisation and rectification of their follies we are inscribing here examples of some scientific discoveries.

Here the humble author of this bio-graphy would like to request the respected readers to study the life of the great saint Trailanga Swami, as described in this book. The history of his voluntary departure from his body, his saintliness beyond the three *gunas* or properties that flesh is subject to, i.e. *Sattva*, *Rajas* and, *Tamas*, the wonderful saint's ever steady health and the power behind his supernatural abilities all these are to be closely studied. Study of this great and holy life, I am sure, will enrich us immensely in the spiritual sense, without any geographical or religious barrier. Further contemplation over this will yield inspirations for us to yearn for the master spirit and the true life beyond life.

As a popular English proverb states, "Lives of great men all remind us we can make our lives sublime". The message is really inspiring for us all. Biographies of great men like Trailanga Swami are undoubtedly a silver lining in the dark clouds of our stupified vision and pent up soul.

In Sanskrit texts too, the great *rishis* also gave their message to us: "*Shrinvantu Vishwe Amritasya Putrah*" —— "You are the children of immortibility, be Immortal!"

We also like to opine that the keen observation of great lives must beget the true and highest meaning of life for us all.

॥ ॐ तत् सत्॥

|| om tat sat ||

Now let this chapter conclude with the following great message from the rishis in their core of hearts!

"ॐ पूर्णमदः पूर्णमिदं पूर्णात्पूर्णमुदच्यते। पूर्णस्य पूर्णमादाय पूर्णमेवावशिष्यते॥

ॐ हरि ॐ। ॐ तत् सत्।

ॐ शान्तिः शान्तिः शान्तिः।

Chapter 12. Disciples of Trailanga Swami

An accurate assessment of the number of devotees that Trailanga Swami had is beyond estimation. No one can ascertain this accurately as it is not possible to know that how many men or women were graced by him publicly or privately, directly or indirectly during his long lifetime. Besides, he never allowed any one of them to stay close to him for a long period except our venerable spiritual mother Shri Shri Shankari Mataji.

Shri Umacharan Mukhopadhyay, one of the Bengali disciples of the holy Trailanga Swamiji who got emanicipation while still living and became free from future births, had mentioned the names of only five disciples in his book. As you may recall, we gently protested against this previously.

At this point we would like to mention some of the other disciples of Swamiji that we came to know from our venerable spiritual mother Shri Shri Shankari Mataji:—

- Swami Kalikananda Saraswati (Kalicharan Swami). He was known as Shri Kalicharan Mishra in his pre-ascetic family life. He was a descedant in the holy family of Shri Jagannath Mishra, father of Mahaprabhu Shri Shri Chaitanyadev. He was a prime disciple of Trailanga Swami.
- Swami Brahmananda Saraswati.
- Swami Bholananda Saraswati.
- Swami Sadananda Saraswati.
- Swami Tripuralinga Saraswati. (The famous Bhaila Baba of Dacca, in East Bengal). The key disciples of Tripuralingaji are also known to us :–
    - Shrimat Swami Neelanandaji
    - Swami Shankaranandaji, and
    - Maharaj Srimat Swami Nareshananda Saraswati, of late the Abbott of Swamibagh Dacca.

- Swami Satchidananda Saraswati — He voluntarily took *samadhi* at the age of almost 200 years at Muktinath, Nepal.
    - This author was fortunate enough to meet Swami Satchidanandaji and one of his disciples Bisuddhanandaji alias Bishu or Vidyasthee in 1928 in Hooghly at the residence of sub-judge Shri Surendranath Sengupta, during their trip of India.
- Swami Satyananda Saraswati — He voluntarily took *samadhi* in the year 1918 at Fateyabod, in Chittagong district)
- Swami Narshimananda Saraswati (Narsimhaji) was a famous *Hatha Yogi*, who followed a particular form of abstract meditation. In the early part of his life, he was under the tutelage of Trailanga Swami who taught him the ins and outs of yoga. It was well-known that he could digest strong venom and poisons, and unfortunately during such a demonstration thereof he died before an audience in Rangoon, Burma in 1923. We received the sad news when Shri Shri Mataji Shankari was on a tour in Burma accompanied by me in the year 1934.
- Swami Kanai Lalji — After converting many devotees into his disciples, Swami Kanai Lalji passed away in Kashmir. He had a disciple Balkaka, a Kashmiri Brahmin who was a high ranked government officer and was a key disciple of Swami Kanai Lalji. I had gotten to know him intimately, and he was helpful enough during Mataji's trip to Amarnath to arrange further amenities for us. He had met Mataji at the famous sanatarium and inn at Pahelgaon. Amarnath, the eternally known enblem of Lord Shiva created by snow gathered up in a mass, was seen by us on a full-moon day of *Shravan Bengali* 1303 (English 1936). Then we went to Balkaka's residence, were welcomed by him, and he was given *diksha* by Shri Shri Shankari Mataji.
- Shri Mangal Das Bhatt Bal Brahmachariji was a Marathi Brahmin who lived in the holy city of Kashi. His spiritual father Trailanga Swami lived the last 80 years of his life in the open courtyard of Mangal Bhattji's residence.
- Mahadev Bhatt — Second younger brother of Shri Mangal Bhatt and
- Shri Krishna Bhatt, his youngest brother.
- Shrimati Amba Devi — Mother of Shri Mangal Bhattji.

- Shri Ram Bhatt — the son of Mahadev Bhatt, nephew of Shri Mangal Bhatt.
- Shri Shri Yogeswari Ma — she was renowned as 'Bhairavi Maa' or 'Brahmani Maa'. She watched Thakur Shri Shri Ramkrisna Paramhansa Dev in his *samadhi* state when she was 26 years of age at the behest of her Guru Trailanga Swami; and she further went on to meet three great sages of Bengal. Having met Shri Ramkrishna, she assured every one of his kith and kin about his divinity, and provided instructions to Shri Ramkrishna on the practice of *tantra*. Later on, Shri Ramakrishna was further instructed by the famous Sage Shri Totapuree at the Kali Temple of Rani Rashmani at Dakshineswar in Advaita Vedanta. Some of the above information might be known to all, but additional details are provided for the benefit of the readers.
- Maa Rajalakshmi Devi (named as Ambalika by her Guru). She was the wife of Shri Kalicharan Mishra and the mother of our spiritual mother Shri Shri Shankari Mataji.
- The celibate renunciate Shri Shri Shankari Mataji, our venerable spiritual mother is the only one living disciple of Baba Trailanga Swami. She was the only child to her parents Shri Kalicharan Mishra and Rajlakshmi Devi. She is a resident of 142, Audhagarbhi, in a *bhajan ashram* as suggested by her Guru. She remains engaged in the worship of Shri Shri Radharaman and her Guru since last 10 years. Even in this old age she goes out on tours. We will share many other details of her sacred life in her biography.
- Shri Kedarnath Bandyopadhyay Vachaspati — Shri Bandyopadhyay was a householder disciple of Shri Trailanga Swami, but an ardent devotee nevertheless. His only son Master Durgadas Bandyopadhyay B.A. pleader was well known to us. He and his wife were disciples of Swami Niranjananda of Haridwar. He lived the life of a householder, engaged as a lawyer by profession. Then he left the legal profession and took on a job in Jabalpur. Afterwards, he gave up the householder life and became a renunciate, withdrawn from society and living in the woods. Later he became established in his own self and then breathed his last. When he came to Mataji to meet her for the first time, Mataji told him that his face was rather familiar to her as he resembled his father. He expressed his deep desire to be accepted as her disciple, and when he mentioned the name of

his father Shri Kedarnath Vachaspati then both of them became highly pleased. "*Atma boijayati putrah*"—Such a son is verily a treasure to his parents! Through his spiritual efforts, not only does he get emanicipated but also provides immense spiritual benefits to his own family and to his Guru. In the book "Maha Patakeer Jeevane Shri Shri Sadguru Leela" authored by one of the disciples of the great Shri Shri Vijaykrishna Swami, the following comments were made about Shri Vachaspati—"The honest pious Brahmin young man Baba Kedarnath (later on he became a disciple of the venerable Shri Trailanga Swamiji) was my classmate. He attracted me deeply for his clarity of religious thought and free heart. I had my own morals and values, and so was mutually respected and thus enriched by his character. It was as if a fountain of love between us spontaneously uprose that soaked us both."

- Shri Ramtaran Bhattacharya was a householder disciple.
- Shri Umacharan Mukhopadhyay — He was Shri Trailanga Swami's last disciple who also lived as family man. He authored a book tittled "Jeevanmukto Swamijir Jeevanee", 42 years after his Guru's demise. We have included the author's own biographic outlines in the 13th chapter of this book.

Note: Apart from the above mentioned disciples, we have referred to a few other disciples and provided brief profiles in different chapters in course of this text.

The author would like to humbly state that the aforementioned list of the disciples of Baba Trailanga Swamiji was authenticated by none other than our spiritual mother Shri Shri Shankari Mataji herself. We do believe many other spiritual aspirants also got valuable spiritual advice from Swamiji.

P.S. The following sages received the guidance of Trailanga Swamiji as a teacher of yoga:-

1) The famous Saint Lokenath Brahmachari of Baridi.

2) Shri Benimadhab Ganguly, and

3) Fakir Abdul Gafurji, as mentioned earlier by us.

We have also mentioned that the intial initiation of Shri Shri Vijaykrishna Goswami was also done by Trailanga Swamiji. The following statements from the biography of Goswamiji that are attributed to Vijaykrishanji himself are quoted below for the benefit of our readers:

'When I was member of the Bharatiya Brahmo Samaj, one day I came across Trailanga Swamiji.

I used to get up at dawn and accompany Swamiji. Sometimes with the progress of hours he used to ask me with silent gestures whether I was hungry. If I replied affirmatively, he used to order any person who he knew to go and bring me food. They respected his order and usually used to bring an excessive amount of food. I had to say that it was impossible for me to eat that whole quantity of food myself, and would ask if he could take a portion of it himself. He would agree and indicate that I feed him myself. He could eat a lot of food. Since he used to eat up the entire quantity of the food with no trouble, I had to keep some of it aside for myself, and would say, "Let me keep aside a portion of food for myself first." With his divine smile he used to write on the soil "*Baccha saccha hai*". Sometimes he used to live under the water of the Ganges and sometimes he would be seen swimming near Manikarnika Ghat. I had to run and cover the distance along the banks to reach him.

One day suddenly he began to sprinkle his own urine on the idol of Maa Kali. When I asked, "*Why are you sprinkling urine on the image of Kali Maa?*" He said, "*Gangodakam*", I asked, "*But why on the idol?*" He replied, "*I am worshiping.*" The temple was then deserted. When some people gathered there I told them that he had sprinkled his urine on the idol saying that it was nothing but the water of the Ganges. They said, "He himself is the embodiment of Lord Shiva; do not criticise him in this way. It is true that he urinates Ganga water." I became immensely astonished on witnessing the faith and devotion that people had in him.

One day while roaming on the strand of the Ganges near Dashashwamedh Ghat he suddenly caught hold of my hand and having broken his vow of silence said, "*I would give you the initial religious text (deeksha).*" I replied, "*What a proposal! Why should I receive religious initiation from you who sometimes sprinkles his urine on the idol of Kali, and sometimes worships Lord Shiva? I am not going to be your disciple, and especially when I am a believer in Brahmoism—the non-dual concept. I don't believe in Gurus.*"

He smiled his usual divine smile and said in Hindi, "*Baccha saccha hai.*" (The child is honest). He further said, "*I do have some deeply significant and confidential reasons behind my intention to give you the initiatory texts. Without a Guru one can not be physically purified. I am not your Guru; he is someone else who will arrive at an appropriate time in the future. But I will make you physically purified.*" Then he gave me three-fold *mantras* and said, *"I am just obeying the command of God to me.*"'

Later, when Goswamiji went to the holy Kashi-dham after becoming a renunciate and having learnt yoga, one day he came across his initiator Trailanga Swami, who exclaimed, "*Kya? yaad hai.*" (What, do you remember?). Entranced in devotion, Vijaykrishna replied, "*Yes, my Guruji.*"

(Extracted from "Probhupaad Bijoy Krishna Goswami", by Amritalal Sengupta).

In his own book, "Ashabateer Upaphyan", Goswamiji wrote (Ashabati was his pseudonym) wrote: Ashabati knelt before Trailanga Swami, touched his feet and said, "Your majesty, I am an ignorant person who knows nothing. Don't be unkind to me. You are an ocean of knowledge and I am coming to your holy vicinity since I am feeling inquisitive and would like to know so many things that are unknown to me. I would like to ask you that who and how many are worthy of worship in this mortal world?"

Trailanga Swami wrote with a piece of stone in Devnagari: "Worshipable is only One. One may worship Him in their own way, and any of His forms but actually all of this worship goes to the Ultimate,'The ONE'. Because God is One, without a second. He is *Shivam.*" Then he was asked what the truth is about Shiva, the husband of Parvati? Swamiji replied, "*Mangalam*". Ashabati asked, "What is His form?" Trailanga Swami replied, "He stays in His devotee's heart as an idol of eternal and divine pleasure."

Ashabati then asked, "Then what is the use of idol worship?"

Trailanga Swami replied, "*Puja* is possible through two methods:

1) *Sabalamban*, and 2) *Niralambaan* i.e. 1) Dependent on a representation, and 2) Independent and formless.

A symbolic, form-based representation of the Supreme via wood or stone or made of clay idols, in a *ghat* (a clay or metal vessel) or a photo, in water, soil, the moon, a tree, a creeper, a river, or a mountain, all these belong to the ways of *Sabalamban*, i.e. dependence. The worship depending on these God-created objects is called *Sabalamban* and this method of worshiping is somewhat inferior. However one has to depend on these methods of worship till one sees or feels *Brahman*, the Supreme formless version. After perceiving *Brahman* directly one no longer needs *Sabalamban*; i.e.

dependance on any object that is a form based symbolic representation like idols or replicas.

2) The prayer hymn (*mantra*) of *Sabalamban Puja* says:

Oh God! Existent in the clay-pot, idol, water, fire, and omnipresent in all the creations of the universe—Salute to thee!

But the *Niralamban* (independent) prayer text goes:

"*Twam Hi! Twam Hi! Twam Hi!*" (Only Thee! Only Thee! Only Thee!).

Sabalamban Puja is akin to a flight of stairs: if caught up in any of them one can perceive the Truth—the Supreme Reality—only after considerable delay."

Ashabati asked, "How can the Truth be realised?" In reply Trailanga Swami did not write anything more. He demonstrated some *yogas* sitting in his *yogasana*.

Ashabati was accompained by a yogi. He said to Ashabati, "Behold! What a spectacular sight! It is as if the full-moon has risen! What a wave of laughter!"

The great Swami controlled his gesture. The yogi and Ashabati left the place after touching Swami's feet in respect.

|| ॐ तत् सत् ||

|| om tat sat ||

Chapter 13. Disciple Shri Umacharan Mukhopadhyay

Shri Umacharan Mukhopadhyay, author of the book, titled "Jeevanmukta Trailanga Swamiji Jeevan Charit" was an employee in a doctor's office in the town of Munger, near Jamalpur in the province of Bihar.

He used to be constantly in a confused state of mind after listening to so many contrasting ideas around religion and spirituality, and especially around how *Sanatana Dharma* elaborated on the the concept of reincarnation and future births, and the Law of Karma—i.e. future pains or pleasure are purely a consequence of one's own acts.

He became increasingly restless when he could not find answers that would reasonably remove the confusion in his mind. He was born in a noble Brahmin family and had a clear conscience, which probably was a blessing due to good karma accumulated from his previous births. His mind was constantly in turmoil thinking about these things, and wanting to get answers. He tried to live in solitude and prayed fervently to God for divine grace so that he could find the right path towards the Supreme Truth.

God, of course, never ignores the call of His true devotees, being omniscient. Many of us hear about this, but how many can perceive, feel it by heart. We can attest though such grace of God is indeed possible and is absolutely true.

He became aware of the sage Trailanga Swami and heard about his remarkable spritual powers. He became convinced that all the confusion in his mind would get clarified only by the grace of Trailanga Swami. Obviously, the Lord above Himself caused such a thought to appear in him.

He went to the holy Kashi-dham in1880 in the month of *Agrahayana*. He visited all the local pilgrimage spots and shrines at first, and then one day finally visited Trailanga Swami in his ashram adjacent to the Benimadhab Dhwaja on the strand of Pancha Ganga Umacharan felt high degree of reverence at the sight of Trailanga Swamiji.

However, he kept quiet and suppressed all the questions that were bubbling within him and went back. Next morning, after taking a bath in the Ganges he came to Swamiji's place, and bowed down and touched his feet.

He stood silently observing the divine appearance of Swamiji. He was thinking about asking a question around 'rebirth' when the Swamiji signalled that he leave the place. He had wished to stay some more time, but Swamiji's devotee Mangal Bhattji asked him to leave the place immediately.

Umacharan could not show disrespect to Swamiji's directive, and so went back quietly with his mind in an agitated state. The next day he went to his ashram again with deep reverence in his mind, but in the afternoon once again had to return due to the same reason.

We know that spiritual aspirants have to face and overcome tough tests before they get any success; and likewise even in the case of Umacharan, such tests were now happening.

He went to Trailanga Swami's ashram for 12 days consecutively, twice every day in the morning and afternoon, but could not ask his questions to Swamiji who repeatedly directed that he leave the ashram. Umacharan began to feel depressed, but he did not give up.

He went to the shrine of Trailanga Swami on the 13th day at morning. After bowing and touching his feet, he stood aside silently thinking and anticipating that he would be turned out of the ashram yet again. In deep sadness he was unable to control his emotions, and so suddenly he burst into tears. Trailanga Swami this time displayed compassion for Umacharan, and said that Umacharan should take a seat near him. The long-desired gesture of affection from Swamiji affected Umacharan deeply, and his tears were pouring out unrestrained.

He literally washed the holy feet of Trailanga Swami with his spontaneous tears. A few moments later Swamiji called Mangal Bhattji and directed him to ask Umacharan to leave the place for then and return the next morning. Umacharan got some solace and felt a bit assured that his hopes might be fulfilled. He went back waiting for the next day break.

With soaring aspirations, the next day Umacharan bathed in the Ganga waters at dawn, and then went to meet the Swamiji with delight in his heart. He touched Swamiji's holy feet with his forehead, and sprinkled the holy dust of Swamiji's venerable feet all over his own body. Umacharan said, "The holy proximity of a holy sage dispersed all worries from my heart; and I felt as if my body and soul were sanctified. I felt something completely new, and perceived an unstained pleasure within."

When Umacharan gazed nonstop at the Swamiji's pleasant and calm face with fascinated eyes, Swamiji signaled to Mangal Bhattji to bring something. His faithful devotee Mangal Bhattji fetched a piece of red ochre, a piece of stone, and a container full of water and said, "Baba instructs you to rub this red ochre."

He (Umacharan) did so till mid-day and then returned home to have his lunch. When he returned to Swamiji's place he was told to do the same thing again, and Umacharan did so without any hesitation.

Sometime later a *brahmachari* came to Swamiji. Swamiji instructed him to write something on the wall in Devnagari with the paste of the red chalk used by Umacharan. The *brahmachari* did accordingly. At dusk, Swamiji ordered Umacharan to keep the paste in a tumbler and leave the place, and with his head bowed in reverence Umacharan quietly complied with the order.

The next morning (on the 15th day) when Umacharan went there after bathing in the Ganges and touched Swamiji's feet, he was again instructed to rub and make the paste. Umacharan wrote in his biography: "While constantly rubbing the red chalk, whenever I slowed down due to my hands aching, with a grim face, the Swamiji would signal to me that I needed to use my hands faster. I used to do so with all my strength, being scared of seeing the Swamiji's grave face."

Umacharan continued to do this for two consecutive days, and each day the *brahmachari* used to write something on the wall with the red ochre paste. After 15 days of this ordeal, Umacharan had become almost numb after extracting all the paste when the day's toil was finished.

The *brahmachari* was unmoved even when Umacharan seemed to be unable to extract red-chalk paste by rubbing the piece of red-chalk with all his might. Besides, his heartfelt wishes and questions for which he came to meet Baba Trailanga Swami remained unasked, even though 28 days had passed in this way.

On the 29th day he went to the Swami, touched his feet and began pondering over the prospect of his visit there, which was still unclear to him as of that morning. He wrote later about what was going on his mind at that moment: "If the Swami brings the mass of red-chalk today also, then what can I do? Both my hands have become almost paralysed. It the Swami refuses to entertain me because of my inability to extract paste from the red-chalk anymore, all my aspirations and labour will go fultile." He wept like a helpless child on thinking about this.

It was as if flash of silver lining in the mass of dark clouds appeared suddenly, startling Umacharan—Trailanga Swami smiled a slight smile and asked through Mangal Bhattji if Umacharan was conversant with

Devnagari. Swamiji became pleased to know that Umacharan could read Devnagari script.

Swamiji took out a bamboo-pipe from his blanket and handed it over Umacharan. He made Umacharan understand through Mangal Bhattji that he has to translate the Devnagari *shlokas* written on the pipe in to Bengali. Umacharan heaved a deep sigh, relieved that he would no longer need to extract paste from the red chalk. He began to translate those Devnagari *shlokas* into Bengali. He took five days to complete the task, and then three more days passed in translating a few more *shlokas*.

The next day in the afternoon Umacharan touched Swamiji's feet and sat down. Swamiji glanced at him gracefully and lay down silently. Umacharan thought that he had nothing to do, so he began to massage and knead the tender legs of the great Swami. When Swamiji said nothing, Umacharan gathered a bit of courage. He decided to put forth the questions that had been churning in his mind to Swamiji. But the Swami got up at dusk and adviced him to arrive in the same hour of the next day. When Umacharan arrived in the next day, Swamiji entered the underground room where he practiced his devotional activities, situated under his *yogasan,* taking Umacharan with him. He used to give initatory prayers (*mantra-deeksha*) to his disciples there in the underground room. Swamiji forbade anybody's presence there and directed Mangal Bhatttaji to enforce his orders.

When Trailanga Swami sat on his seat, Umacharan sat near him. To fulfill his devotee's ardent desires after passing a long ordeal, he began to speak in an affectionate but firm voice, "My son! Why are you so confused about the answers to your questions that you have brought to me? Your ignorance is the root of your confusions. Ignorance does not help overcome doubts. Doubts orginate from ignorance. Only true knowledge can eradicate ignorance. My son! Just listen to me! The omniscient sages and *rishis* perceived the Truth only after years of intense austerities and the dedicated practice of yoga. They had probed into the Absolute Truth and revealed their findings only so that we opened our eyes. Their judgement is beyond any doubt. Perception of the Ultimate Truth is possible only when the soul is in union with the Supreme Spirit, in the fourth state (*Turiya*) of the consciousness.

The Truth perceived by the *rishis* can never be doubted. Better know and accept it as the Supreme Truth tested through eternity. Know undoubledly that all the living beings have to go through the cycle of birth and death.

According to their righteousness or any sinful acts they have commited previously, they get the fruits of happiness or suffer from miseries in every succeeding rebirth. Sincerity and firmness in undergoing the austerities of full *Brahmacharya* gives the rare strength of memory in the sincere devotee such that he becomes able to know his past, present, and future state of life due to the supernatural powers that get acquired.

But how it can be within the purview of the opposite character of a man? How many actually desire to know these secrets? Only one who devotes himself wholeheartedly with physical purity and practices *Brahmacharya* throughout one's life can understand this. Where is the gurantee that you are going to believe all my statements and become convinced? However as you have come to me with an inquisitive mind and undergone a very stern test sucessfully, I will make you understand the doctrine of prior–birth and show every detail of it before your mortal eyes."

Swamiji, with his divine power of vision, said, "Initially I am going to tell you about some incidents of your early life that would be unknown to all here, except you. If you find them to be credible and true, then you will find it easier to believe my words. I will also tell you details later that are not even known to you, and for which you have come to me like an ordinary student. You will find each and every word from me to be true then; it is obvious. Just try to understand that when a man takes a rebirth, he must be endowed with the three-fold intutions and ingredients—separately combined with different molecules that form a new body. One who had played musical instruments in his past life must be able to play music in his new life. Likewise, a thief in the past life will have a tendency to steal things in this life. But one who kept good campany and received the grace of super souls can convert their lives into a better state in the future. Ratnakara, the robber and the looter, only became Rishi Valmiki by the noble influence of Narada Muni, and only when he devoted himself in spiritual austerities in order to reach the Supreme Truth. If you think deeply, you will realise that if there is nothing like the after life, then God Himself could not be worshiped as the Graceful Almighty."

Everybody opines that the extent of injustice doled out by God Himself is worse than even the worst tyrant could possibly deal out. "*MySon! Don't think at only the gross levels! Take your mind into the subtle depths. If mortal beings were subject only to birth, then they do not need be born again! The word 'afterworld' would have been meaningless, and then why would there be so many differences between one man and another? Such as the difference between a king and his subjects, a rich man and a pauper, one who rides in a palanquin and one who carries it, between a priest and a sweeper? Why there is such a difference between a yogi and one who enjoys sensory pleasures? There are differences between a patient who is suffering and one with sound health, people absorbed in enjoying riches and luxury, and others who are indifferent to mundane matters. Why do some have to live a life of hardship, while others live in mirth and happiness? Why are there so many dissimilarities or differences in the states of one man versus another? No body gets punished without committing any crime. Does God have no sense in diffferentiating between good and bad? It is impossible. No one other than the Eternal God has the ability to judge such matters. These are beyond the purview of ignorant people. Lives of men are so sharply repugnant due to their own acts in their past lives. They reap the consequences of what they sow. As a mirror reflects a pleasant face equally pleasant, a smiling face with its immaculate smile, and a gruesome face looks appalling, likewise a man's righteousness and sinful conduct are mirrored in the happiness, or lack thereof, in his next life. One who performs sinful acts goes further down in his future births. On the other hand those who are righteous and live pious, spiritual lives deserve elevation of their souls, and this is eternally true. If, my son, you do not commit any sin, nobody can punish you! Just like a person with a disease needs treatment from a physician, but one in good state of health does not."*

Swamiji, who had divine realization, used to teach the Eternal Truth that was attained by him to his disciples for their spiritual upliftment. That is the reason he was conveying the same message to Umacharan: "*My child, always think of your own legacy, the form, education, intelligence, nature inherited by you, and then you will know what kind of a man you had been in your past life. You can visualise the results of your past life, and you know the degree of good or bad actions performed by you in this present life. Do good actions and get good rewards! Because as you sow, so shall you reap. Your activities in life will indicate to you the nature of your next re-birth, its source. You have become a Brahmin owing to your piety in your last life.*

On the other hand, if you were not righteous and did not do good deeds, in the next birth you might end up in a much worse life as a man, or you can even be downgraded to the life of an animal. We can clearly realize this from the example of 'Jada Bharata' (motionless, inactive Bharata: Bharata was an ancient king who lived a devout life and thus achieved spiritual progress. However, in his last stage of life—*Vanaprastha*, as a hermit in the the woods, one day he ended up saving the life of a new-born fawn whose mother breathed her last after giving birth having been chased by a lion. He became extremely attached to the fawn and forgot his spiritual activities. Even while dying, in the last moments of his life he was continually absorbed in the thoughts of his beloved fawn.

As a result, in his next life he became a deer, though he was able to recollect his prior life as a result of his *tapas* and merits accumulated in the previous life. Gradually, his life as a deer, lived in the vicinity of a *rishi's* ashram, ended; and then again in his next birth he became a Brahmin who remembered his past lives. To avoid descending any further in his next life, he abstained from all earthly affairs, lived an inactive life, and spoke gibberish. As a result he was called Jada Bharata).

If one lives normally, he will become normal as he was in his prior birth. Thus, you can guess the future nature of your life and birth while existing in this present life. You do not have to ask anybody. Now I am going to tell you—something significant that will reaffirm your belief and knowledge."

Then the omniscient Mahayogi Trailanga Swami began to reveal to Umacharan his knowledge of all the intimate details of Umacharan—about his name, father's name, facts about his family members, how many rooms there were in his residence, number of trees and plants in the garden, the exact location of the pond etc. with complete command over the reality.

Umacharan's astonishment exceeded all bounds. The Swami narrated Umacharan's life story of this present life, as well as all the details of his past life. He disclosed that Umacharan was a Brahmin and a famous *zamindar* (landlord) in his previous birth. At the very end, he informed him that, three *shlokas* (verses in Devnagari) written by Umacharan himself in his previous life still existed on the wall of his bedroom with a south facing door on the first floor of his residence. The *shlokas* read thus:

वसांसि जीर्णानि यथा विहाय नवानि गृण्हति नरोऽपराणि।

तथा शरीराणि विहाय जिर्णान्य न्यानि संयाति नवानि देही॥

vasāṁsi jīrṇāni yathā vihāya navāni gṛṇhati naro'parāṇi |
tathā śarīrāṇi vihāya jirṇānya nyāni saṁyāti navāni dehī ||

(The Bhagavad Gita – 2:22)

Translation: *Just as a man giving up old worn out garments accepts other new clothes, in the same way the embodied soul giving up old and worn out bodies verily accepts new bodies.*

रुचीनां वैचित्र्यादृजुकुटिल नानापथजुषां।

नृणामेको गम्यस्त्वमसि पयसामर्णव ईव॥

rucīnāṁ vaicitrayādṛjukuṭila nānāpathajuṣāṁ |
nṛṇāmeko gamyastvamasi payasāmarṇava īva ||

Translation: *Just as different rivers and streams go through different ways and yet the sea is their final resting place, likewise there are many ways to worship God, but the ultimate destination is You—the Supreme Soul.*

(Shiva Mahimna Stotra—*Shloka* 7)

चिन्मयस्या प्रमेयस्य निर्गुणस्य शरीरिणाः।

साधकानां हितार्थाय ब्रह्मणः रुपकल्पना॥

cinmayasyā prameyasya nirguṇasya śarīriṇāḥ |
sādhakānāṁ hitārthāya brahmaṇaḥ rupakalpanā ||

Translation: *The Supreme Consciousness cannot be measured, has no attributes or form; however for the welfare of the devotees He appears in many forms.*

(Kularnava Tantra)

In later days Umacharan got confirmation that everything revealed by the great sage regarding his past life was absolutely correct. After that, he had no doubt about the Law of Karma and rebirths

Continuously being present in the Swamiji's company removed all confusion and doubts from the mind of Umacharan. He also got a purified mind full of enlightened wisdom by the grace of Trailanga Swami. Days passed by, and then one day his cup of fortune flowed over. He was initiated and given *mantra deeksha* by the gracious Trailanga Swami.

He had the opportunity to learn from his Guru, and got spiritual instructions given to him daily. One day Swamiji said, "*God has provided man with the greatest might and man is the greatest of all other animals. Man can move and speak due to God's grace—without which corporal body becomes inactive and immovable. Just see, God is prevading in man but, entranced by the glitter of earthly pleasures, man does not remember Him regularly, and abstains from the efforts to achieve God. By sincere endeavour and quest, man can beget Him, who is always existent within his own self.*"

Umacharan asked, "*Baba, (Father) is it true that one can see God?*" Trailanga Swami replied, "*Obviously! He can indeed be seen. Would you like to see Him?*" With folded hands Umacharan replied, "*Oh my Lord! You are ever gracious, be so kind as to fulfil my desires.*"

In the dead of that night Trailanga Swami entered into his underground prayer room. He asked Umacharan, "*Go and take a look at the stone idol of Kali (Mangal Gauri) that exists in the temple.*" Umacharan followed his instructions and saw the stone idol standing on the altar as always, towards the west and to the back to his Guru. Afterwards when Umacharan took his seat, Trailanga Swami went deep into meditation. Trailanga Swami became absolutely still and quiet, as if there were no life in him; and Umacharan felt as if he was viewing his Guru's statue in front of him, but he stayed still gazing in awe without moving. Time flowed quietly by, and after a while the Swami broke his silence and then with deep devotion prayed to the Godess Kali. Before he could even blink his eyes, Umacharan felt the room become full of divine effulgence and an unusual fragrance. Umacharan, in his awestruck state, saw the immobile stone idol of Maa Kali descend the steps slowly and at last stand in front of him. By the grace of his Guru, Umacharan was able to see the exquisite beauty of Maa Kali—the Supreme Mistress of the Universe. He sat there dumbstruck staring at the unimaginably graceful and tender Mother.

Trailangawami said, "*Umacharan, my child, go and check if the stone idol is still standing as usual on the altar of the temple.*"

Umacharan rushed above to the temple and was astounded to see that the altar no longer had the idol. When he came back, Swamiji said, "*Umacharan, my son! What nonsense are you doing? You have forgotten to bow down and touch the feet of the Mother of the Universe who has graced you just now by revealing Herself to you!*" Umacharan immediately touched the feet of the Mother, and perceived the divine feet of the Mother to be softer than the petal of a flower, and felt a shudder of ecstacy run through his body. Umacharan's heart filled with unbounded bliss to see the divine serenity of the Mother. He had no more desires left, and his life became completely successful because of the grace of his Guru!!

A few minutes later, the Mother of the Universe returned, on Trailanga Swami's respectful sign, taking tender steps like a little girl. Umacharan followed and saw Her standing on the altar just like She had been before. Umacharan was completely out of senses, as if he had plunged in to some fathomless, bottomless wonder! Trailanga Swami removed him from his trance-like state by saying, "*God had induced the divine consciousness (Brahma Chaitanya) in us—we are no longer stones, but we become inactive like a static and stationary stone when that very power leaves us after death. But, oh my son, a sadhaka of higher level who is called as 'Siddha Saddha Sadhak (A spiritual aspirant who has attained perfection) can induce consciousness to that inactive matter easily at his will, and bring it to life!!*"

Umacharan continued staying there for some more days after that. One day Trailanga Swami told him, "*Umacharan, my son! Now you need to go back to your home. You are a married man and therefore you have responsibilities to your family. You had taken a leave of 3 months but have ended up staying here for a long 8 months. You still are working in a job that continues till date. Go back to your home and do your duties, but at the same time remember to continue your spiritual practices with utmost sincerety, apart from your mundane activities. You must achieve spiritual success!*"

Umacharan was deeply sad about leaving the divine company of his great Guru, but he had no choice but to follow the orders of his Guru. The next day, Umacharan left for his work place Munger and then rejoined his office and resumed his job. He lived a long life after retiring from his job. Afterwards he went to Chandan Nagar and lived there with his family. He was originally a resident of Bansberia (Bangshabati) in the district of Hooghly district. Umacharan, the devoted and pious disciple of Trailanga Swami, who received his Guru's grace and that of Maa Kali, finally left for his heavenly abode in 1932.

॥ ॐ तत् सत् ॥

|| om tat sat ||

Note

1) In the next 14th chapter we are going to describe the holy biography of our venerable religious mother Shri Shri Shankari Mataji.
2) The spiritual advice from the holy Trailanga Swami and Mataji and their messages will be published in separate volume later on.

Chapter 14. Biography of Shri Shri Shankari Mataji—the Celibate Ascetic

सर्वमङ्गलमाङ्गल्ये शिवे सर्वार्थसाधिके।

शरण्ये त्र्यम्बके गौरि नारायणि नमोऽस्तु ते॥

sarvamaṅgalamāṅgalye śive sarvārthasādhike |
śaraṇye trayambake gauri nārāyaṇi namostute ||

(Shri Durga Saptashati, 11:10)

Translation: *Salutations to You, O Naarayani, who is the Auspiciousness in All the Auspiciousness, Auspiciousness Herself and complete with all the Auspicious attributes.*

मूकं करोति वाचालं पङ्गुं लङ्घयते गिरिम्।

यत्कृपा तमहं वन्दे परमानन्दमाधवम्॥

mūkaṁ karoti vācālaṁ paṅguṁ laṅghayate girim |
yatkṛpā tamahaṁ vande paramānanda mādhavam ||

(Gita Dhyaana Shloka 8)

Translation: *I salute Lord Madhava, by Whose Grace the dumb can become eloquent, and the lame can cross over mountains.*

The author has been the sole, humble disciple of the eternally graceful and beloved spiritual mother Shri Shri Shankari Mataji for the last 18 years at a stretch, a case of divine grace reaching the meek spontaneously. He is quoting verbatim in this chapter, the stories from the holy life of Shri Shri Shankari Mataji, as narrated by Mataji herself.

The author feels that her life is a mirror that contains the reflection of her spiritual father, the holy Trailanga Swami. The Mahaguru had instilled within his beloved disciples all the ingredients of the spiritual discipline that he himself possessed. Thus our holy Mataji's life and spiritual activities echoed the messages—of her great Gurudev's holy life and work. Trailanga Swami guided her life with the aim of emanicipation and freedom from further rebirth, and thus one can easily perceive the magnanimity of Trailanga Swami within the life of Shri Shri Shankari Mataji.

Mataji's life is a perfect representation of the life of her Guru, complete with unbroken spiritual austerities and steadfast attention towards God—The Absolute. Her life and spiritual activities were the epitome of selfless devotion towards God. She is still alive continuing her steady spiritual activities, even though she is free from the possibility of any further rebirth. In many contexts, she used to quote her Gurudev's messages and just repeat essential natural aspects of the holiness of Trailanga Swami. Our endeavour will be to describe her as we see her. We are indeed aware of some of our own flaws, and we do realise that it is simply impossible to write biographies of great souls without ourselves being at the lofty levels that they are at. Yet we know the biography of Shri Shri Shankari Mataji would undoubtedly bring divine happiness to her devotees and disciples. We hope that despite all the mistakes and incompleteness in this biography, it will be regarded as the torch that shows the path to freedom for countless Indians and people in the world, whether they be men or women, and be able to guide their soul to the avenue of piety and peace.

|| ॐ तत् सत् ||

|| om tat sat ||

ॐ शान्तिः शान्तिः शान्तिः ||

om śāntiḥ śāntiḥ śāntiḥ ||

Shri Shri Shankari Mataji with her disciples at the Haridwar Kumbha Mela in 1938, when she was 111 years old. To extreme left is Swami Paramanand Saraswati.

The Holy Birth of Shri Shri Shankari Mataji

Our spiritual mother, the beloved and divine Shri Shri Shankari Mataji is the only known living disciple of the great sage Baba Trailanga Swami, who was widely known as *Mahayogeshwar* (The Great Yogi) and the Living Vishwanath of the holy Kashidham. She was born in the holy city of Kashi-dham. She is a renunciate having taken a lifelong vow of celibacy, and her parents were also disciples of Trailanga Swami.

Shri Kalikananda Mishra (*Kalikananda Swami*) was the father of our spiritual mother Shri Shri Shankari Mataji. His father was Shri Hari Narayan Mishra. His ancestral birth place was in the famous Mishra Gram (Dattarail Thakur Bazar) P.O. Dacca South, and Dacca 24 Parganas, in the district of Srihatta within the former undivided Bengal. Currently, the place belongs to Bangladesh, separated from the Indian Territory after partition of Bengal.

The '*Mishra Vansha*' (the Mishra clan) of that place became famous due its famous descendant, the holy lord Shri Chaitanya Mahaprabhu. His father Shri Jagannath Mishra and his forefathers belonged to that clan. Our religious mother venerable Shri Shri Shankari Mataji also belongs to that blessed clan. She is the only daughter of Shri Kalicharan Mishra, and her mother's name is Ambalika Devi. Ambalika Devi was the daughter of a family who lived in the town of Shantipur in Bengal. Shri Shri Shankari Mataji took birth on the auspicious lunar day (*Tithi*) of *Ram Navami* (The lunar day which corresponds to the one in which Shri Ramachandra, the incarnation of Lord Vishnu took birth) on a Thursday, in the month of *Chaitra* in March 1827 when India was still under British rule.

Note: Fortunately, a temple has been erected on the very land on which Mataji took birth at the eastern adjacent part of the court-yard of Mangal Bhattji in Kashi-dham. The following idols, carved in white-marble, of a few deities and sages are installed there in the temple:

1) Gayatri Devi
2) Dattatreya (tri-headed), the *Aadi* (first) or *Juna* (old) *Sanyasi* (Ascetic) Guru
3) World famous Jagatguru (world-teacher) Bhagavata avatar (an incarnation) Shri Shri Adi Shankaracharya
4) Swami Brahmanandaji—Founder of this temple, however he was not one of the disciples of Trailanga Swami. He was a

Dasanami sanyasi (belonging to the 'ten-names' order). Lately, his Marathi daughter and devotee Parvati Maa looks after the activities and affairs of this temple.

5) Rishi Yagnavalkya and his two wives

6) Katyayani, and

7) Maitreyi Devi

Kalicharan Mishra, father of Shankari Mataji, was highly spiritually inclined and was indifferent and detached from mundane matters since his early days. With the advent of youth, he chose to walk away from starting a family life, due to his spiritual inclinations and tendencies from his previous births and heredity.

After visiting many different places he finally reached the holy Kashi and Shivpuri (dwelling place of Lord Shiva), where he came across Mahayogeshwar Trailanga Swami and received his holy and benevolent grace.

As per the scriptures, the attainment of the Absolute while living in this world in a physical body requires the grace, benevolence, and guidance of a real spiritual teacher (Guru). It is indeed an unquestioned and perpetual truth, and is in accordance with *Sanatana Dharma*.

The great holy sage Rishi Vasistha was the spiritual Guru of Lord Ramachandra, whereas Rishi Sandipani was the spiritual teacher to Lord Shri Krishna. One can attain the grace and benevolence of such Gurus only when the time is appropriate. It is attainable only by sincere and fervent longing for God and incessant prayer to the Almighty.

Baba Trailanga Swami ordered Kalicharan to marry, even though he had previously decided to remain a life-long celibate, keeping himself away from the bondage of family life as he felt that life would not allow him to fulfil his loftiest ambition of reaching God. Shri Shri Gurudev with his divine foresight saw the details of Kalicharan's many previous lives, and then decided that he should live the life of a married man.

Kalicharan was reassured that his long cherished desire to reach God would not be in vain or get affected by his marriage. Thus having been reassured by his spiritual father, he got married to a bride who came from a famous family from Shantipur in Nadia District. The couple began to live in the holy Kashi, detached from their matrimonial life in its true sense.

After some days, while Shri Shri Mataji was conceived and was in the womb of her mother, her father Kalicharan, out of his intensive aversion to wordly matters devoted his self to the feet of his Guru and begged to be initiated as *sanyasi* and become a renunciate. The Gurudev said, "*Kalicharan, my son! This is your last life in the world as a human being. You will become successful in achieving divine grace and all your desires that are reflected in your activities will perish. Then you will become a liberated soul. Just as no paddy plant can grow from fried paddy, similarly the fire of divine knowledge will reduce all your lustful activities that distract from the pursuit of the Supreme into heaps of ashes and prevent any further rebirth for you.*"

Kalicharan, father of Shankari Mataji, then further expressed his mental anguish and asked, "*Baba, are you going to put me up in any further captivity?*"

Swamiji said in reply, "*See Kalicharan! Can anybody keep in capitivity any pious soul, longing sincerely for emanicipation? Never! Only a person who forgets himself can be locked up into captivity. Just realise that there is Brahmashakti (Infinite Power) within each and every man. One can get liberated by that power, at His will. But mind you, within a man there exist both the opposite type of forces—philistine and human consciousness. The first one signifies animal instinct and the latter denotes humanity. When a man egolessly submits as a refugee to God, only then can he achieve true knowledge and God. On the other hand, submission to primal instincts leads to unavoidable bondage in the form of family life and other earthly sufferings. A silk worm looms a snare with its own saliva and ultimately it gets trapped in it and cannot fly freely. Again, with its natural transformation of body it gets sharp denture and wings. Then it cuts open the net and flies in the form of a beautiful butterfly. Kalicharan, you yourself have built your net like a silk worm. But you can also get free from it you cut the net open and fly away, like a free butterfly with its colored wings.*"

Kalicharan said, "Baba, how can it be possible for me to cut through the net without your graceful blessings?" The Swami said, "*Kalicharan, my child, now you can become a renunciate and pursue spiritual austereties. According to natural process, almost each and every man has to be born in the womb of mother. In ancient days, getting a child based on mental focus was possible. Over the course of time, due to loss of spiritual powers, it now depends on sexual coition. Under the unsurpassable illusory influence of Mahamaya, (Godess of Illusion) they forget about God. In the gestation period the fetus stays hanging upside down with the face and folded hands and in a supine condition. In this position, the being sees his sinful past and comes to know that in the next stage, in the prison of life ceaseless sufferings await it. For this it prays for the Almighty's mercy and longs for Him after intense spiritual austerities.*

After birth, some of men become attracted to material and sensory pleasures and without attachment to God have to take birth in many successive lives and suffer. Some cut up the snare of attractions and illusion of family life and earthly pleasures. Having given up all material desires they then become renunciates. Just think, my son! Inded a lotus grows in the filth of a stagnant pond, however afterwards it leaves all these behind it and through the sun–rays and carbon–assimilation (photo-systhesis), it blooms in profound splendour. Then its fragrance spreads in the air and impregnates the world with its sweet scent before merging finally. My child! You have also taken birth in this world. But bloom like an immaculate lotus, enrich the world with pious deeds and finally merge into eternity."

Swamiji added, "*Just take it for granted; who really is a husband, a wife, a son, or a daughter? We have come alone, and we will leave alone. We had no possessions while being born, and we will have nothing with us when we depart from this mortal world. Only our deeds and spiritual gains will be with us during our journery to the afterworld. We all have to suffer according to our virtue or vices of the previous birth.*"

Soon after that, Kalicharan informed his wife of his plans, and adviced her to depend on the grace of their Gurudev and took the life of an ascetic with the name of Kalikanandaji. He relocated to the tranquil solitude of the Himalayas to pursue his spiritual austerities undisturbed, on the command of his Guru. Shri Kalikanandaji was the dearest and primary disciple of Trailanga Swami. Thus, he passed a long time span in intense austerities in the lap of the Himalayas. He stayed at the Chandi Pahar (Chandi Hills) near Haridwar for a considerable period. He used to visit Trailanga Swami in the holy Kashi-dham on the rare occasions that he received the command to do so from his Guru. A few other renunciate disciples of Trailanga Swami, namely Brahmanandaji, Bholanandaji (Bholanath), Sadanandaji also were in the same vicinity in the Himalayas. Among them, Bholanandaji often used to come and be in Guru Trailanga Swami's proximity. We also heard from our spiritual mother Shri Shri Shankari Mataji that her father Shri Kalikanandaji was able to move around at will in his subtle (invisible) body!

After her husband Kalikanandaji gave up family life and became a renunciate, Ambalika Devi took refuge at the holy feet of Trailanga Swami. She was provided a small room as accomodations, located adjacent to eastern part of Mangal Bhattji's residence. The latter was a Marathi Brahmin and a life long devotee and disciple of Trailanga Swami. She dwelt there under the affectionate care and watch of Trailanga Swami. Swamiji blessed her and anointed her with a new name—'Maa Ambalika'.

Shri Shri Shankari Mataji, our venerable spiritual mother, was born in the auspicious Ram Navami Tithi in the year 1827 in Kashi at her Guru's place. After the period of her physical impurity due to the birth of her daughter was over, Ambalika Devi dedicated her newborn baby at the lotus feet of her Guru. By her Guru's grace, she could clearly understand that it was her Guru's intention that had arranged the place for her to bring forth the baby near her Guru and the holy waters of the Ganges in Kashi-dham. Trailanga Swami affectionately gazed at the newborn baby and opined thus: "*The future of this baby is bright. This baby who took birth in an auspicious moment will be able to save Indians and the people of the world from ignorance and the degradation of humanity.*"

He advised Ambalika Devi to bring up the Goddess-like child with due care. Some days later Trailanga Swami said to her, "*Your daughter will be given initiation (deeksha) and will receive proper education from me. She will remain a lifelong celibate and adopt Brahmacharya (austerities of an ascetic) as her holy mission in life. In due course of time she will acquire immense spiritual powers and Vibrath of yoga. Over the course of her lifetime she will provide benediction for the spiritual and metaphysical development of countless people. Oh Mother! Do not worry about her prospects in life.*" Assured by this, Ambalika Devi began to bring up her daughter with due care, as adviced by her Guru.

The Guru Trailanga Swami and the Childhood of Mataji

In her childhood, Mataji once got a severe attack of small pox to the point it appeared as if her very life was at stake. Her mother Ambalika Devi, inspite of her extraordinary powers of yoga, was crying bitterly sitting at the place where her daughter's head was laid. Mataji was still concious. She said to her mother, "*Mother! My dear mother! Why are you crying? Can't you see Swamiji passing his soothing hand over my body?*"

The mother said, "*What, where is he? I can't see him!*" Mataji took her mother's hand and said, "*Mother! Look, he is there.*"

Ambalika could see her Guru and hear him, "*Don't worry, my mother! Your daughter Shankari will get well very soon. Death cannot touch her at this time.*"

Ambalika heard her Guru's assurance but soon could not see him anymore. He had disappeared in the meantime. Usually at that hour Swamiji would not go anywhere outside the ashram. When Ambalika Devi went to his place, she found out that her Guru did not at all move from his place. He had spent the entire day in intense meditation. He was omniscient and thus there was doubt that he appeared before them in his subtle holy body.

There was a room that was rented out in Kashi adjacent to the east of the ashram area where Ambalika Devi lived with her baby daughter. There was a large wooden image of Rama. Mataji loved that image deeply and used to worship it with flowers and water daily. She did not know any games to play or even any sports. One day she suddenly started wondering as to why had she been a mere wooden doll.

She felt that she should worship Swamiji with offerings of flower and water made at his feet. She fetched water from the Ganges in a small pitcher from the Pancha Ganga Ghat. Returning home, she noticed that in the meanwhile her mother had left towards the ashram to serve her Gurudev with devotion. Then Mataji got ready to go to the ashram by herself to offer flowers and water at Swamiji's holy feet. Suddenly to her surprise she saw that in the place of the wooden image of Ramchandra, which seemed to have disappeared, there was Swamiji himself sitting there with a tender smile on his face. He said to Mataji, "*I have come. Oh my little mother, worship me as you like.*" Then Mataji garlanded Swamiji and prayed to him, and a few minutes later she clearly heard the following:

Jai Jai Maa, Jai Jai Khushali!

Kalyan Karo Go Maa Janani Kaali!

Translation: Victory to Mother! Victory to the Mother who is Supreme Happiness!! Please shower blessings, Oh my Mother Kali!

Immediately Mataji went into an intense meditative trance, losing all consciousness of the outside world. Regaining consciousness, she found herself in her own room, and she could not remember where she had actually been, and Swamiji had already disappeared from there. Later on when she went to Swamiji's ashram, much to her astonishment, she found the garland that she had offered to her Guru completely intact around her Guru's neck. Swamiji was then completely submerged in intense meditation. When he emerged from his meditative state, Mataji asked him, "*Baba, who garlanded you?*" Trailanga Swami replied, "*My little mother, it was you.*" On hearing this, Mataji became awestruck into silence, and tears of joy rolled down her face.

(3)

Another true incident is narrated below for our reader's benefit:

One day when Mataji was around 8 to 10 years old, Trailanga Swami took her with him while going for a bath in the Ganges. He asked her to sit on the flight of steps on Pancha Ganga Ghat while he himself took a dip under the water. He submerged under the water and went out of sight for a long time. Then he emerged and indicated that Shankari Mataji should also take a dip in the Ganges water. Mataji became panic stricken. She said, "*Baba, I don't know how to swim, I might drown.*" Signalling with his hands Trailanga Swami indicated that, *"I am with you and so you don't have to be scared. Come with me."*

Mataji then came down and reached the Swami, and then proceeded to hang on Swamiji's back, putting her hands around his neck firmly. Swamiji dived under the water with the little Mataji with him on his back. Then due to the divine touch of Swamiji, Mataji perceived something extraordinary—with sudden divine vision Mataji clearly saw a heavenly room under the current of the river.

She found Trailanga Swami sitting in that room, in front of her where she herself seemed to be sitting. Trailanga Swami asked Mataji, "*Can you guess what place you have come to?*" Mataji replied, "*I see a new type of house here.*" A little girl who seemed to be around 8 to 10 years old was standing in front of them. Mataji asked Swamiji, "*Baba, who is she?*" Swamiji replied, "*She is Bhagavati Shankari Maa (Goddess Shankari), bow your head before her and touch her feet.*" Mataji did accordingly.

Then again Swamiji asked Shankari Mataji, "*My little mother, once again take a minute to look around at where you are right now. Just tell me what you feel; are we still under the holy water of the river?*" Mataji with her childish innocence said, "*Baba, I am seeing divine houses here; where is Mother Ganga? Why can't I see her?*"

Swamiji said, "*Just try to feel with your hand.*" Mataji followed the instructions and then responded, "*It is all water here.*", and after a short while found herself to be back, sitting on land on the flight of steps down the Panchaganga Ghat; and saw the Swamiji himself happily taking his bath in the Ganges.

After his dips were over they came back to the ashram; and sometime later Mataji asked Swamiji, "*Baba, what was the place where we went to a little while ago?*" Swamiji in reply said, "*My little mother, that was Nashikam Dham (A place that is removed from earthly desires). One can go there only after performing duties free from material desires and earthly lust. You are an innocent girl without any earthly passion and it is because of this purity of heart you were able to go there easily and with your spiritual insight saw your ownself.*" It was possible by the blessings of her Guru, there is no doubt.

At that time Mataji was a simple little girl, unable to naturally understand everything like others. But we can infer that at a very tender age Mataji had her spiritual insight opened up by the divine touch of Trailanga Swami, akin to the opening of her third-eye, the eye of knowledge. Since then she could perceive life vibrant in each and every part of creation like leaves, creepers, and trees. By Swamiji's grace she can still clearly remember all these sweet and sacred memories without any confusion. It is because of all the good deeds and spiritual austerities performed in former lives that when a seeker reaches such a state of conciousness, then he never will deviate from the ultimate goal. He will devote himself incessantly to further spiritual austerities under the holy proximity and guidance from above.

Devotional Practices and Spiritual Austerities of Yoga in Mataji's Childhood

Trailanga Swami, the spiritual Guru to Mataji's parents, initiated Mataji with the *deeksha* on the auspicious day of *Akshaya Tritiya* (The third lunar day of the fortnight when the moon is waxing, in the Bengali month—*Baisakhi*—the 1st month of the Bengali Calender (in 1839). It is believed that any activity begun on that day will be successful and permanent) and asked her to adopt the vow of '*Maha Brahmacharya*' (Lifelong celibacy and pursuit of the Supreme Reality via spiritual austerities).

He invested her with the sacred thread according to the Vedic rites. At present there is a cave-like chamber called *Sadhan Prakostha* (chamber for devotional austerities) under the altar and the seat where Trailanga Swami used to sit. He used to deliver his talks on spiritual processes for his disciples to follow and confer *Upadesa Deeksha* on them there. Swamiji imparted lesson on yoga to Mataji in that very chamber for twelve more years.

Without any hesitation and with a smile on her face, Mataji went about fulfilling that great vow of *Brahmacharya* according to her Guru's instructions for long long period of time. Inspite of living in a human habitation, Mataji would only look at the faces of her mother and spiritual father, but never looked at anything else, not even at the sun or the moon. Swamiji provided her with everything that she required so that she could observe her spiritual practices without any disturbance.

There was a tunnel that existed, that reached the *ghats* of the Ganges from underground chamber of the ashram; her mother Ambalika Devi used to be Mataji's guide while passing through that tunnel to reach the Ganga every day before dawn and at dusk so that she could have her bath in complete solitude, away from the eyes of anyone else.

After the departure of Trailanga Swami, the British government had the tunnel blocked permanently, to prevent the nefarious activities of some goons in Kashi who used to appear and rob rich visitors, for which they had dug some tunnels in few areas of Kashi. Those goons were quite a nuisance during those days. At present the city is safe with the introduction of electric lights present everywhere in the alleys, houses, bathing *ghats* of Kashi.

Visitors to Kashi in the future would be able to see that underground chamber where Mataji practiced her spiritual activities like her Master, if they requested permission from the present abbot of the ashram Shri Mangal Bhattji. It would be wise of them to carry a flashlight to have a clear view of the underground chamber. At the east of the fence encircling Swamiji's altar, a long and wide wooden plank can be found, removal of which will lead the visitors to the flights of steps going down to the cave-like chamber.

Mataji's mother Ambalika Devi used to bring her food once a day only after dusk. The following dietary-habits were strictly followed by Mataji, as per the instructions of her spiritual father Trailanga Swami.

1) For the first four years of her practice — from 12 to 16 years of age — the diet was that of only fruits.

2) For the next four years — from 16 to 20 years of age — the food consisted of only boiled radish and milk.

3) For the final four years — 20 to 24 years of age — a handful of rice and milk used for her worship

Shri Shri Shankari Mataji observed long twelve years of *Brahmacharya* in this strict manner, as per the instructions of Baba Trailanga Swami, only taking food once a day and continuing intense spiritual practices. Quite often Trailanga Swami used to go to the underground cave-chamber to impart further spiritual knowledge and to teach his disciple Shankari Mataji. Swamiji used to break his vow of silence for this purpose, and at the sight of his divine presence, Mataji used to go into deep states of divine contemplation.

Only a few fortunate people can reach that plane and enjoy such divine bliss! Being in this state most of the time, Mataji used to be quite lost in enjoying the bliss of Supreme Consciousness and knowledge of true God, to the extent that she did not even notice the passing of time. During such a tender age, influence of fickleness of mind is quite natural, but her mind was completely merged into the Supreme and thus she was beyond any mundane issues or worries. She simply did not have the problem that all others face, which is: "Why is the mind so agitated?" Suffice to say that she is indeed a divine soul who realised the truth that due to deviation of thought from the divine Creator, all agitations of mind occur.

She passed long twelve years of strict spiritual activities, almost as if unnoticed. Then following her Guru's instruction, she emerged from the small underground chamber when she was twenty-four years old. Readers are gently requested to pay attention to how important and significant was the proximity of Maha Yogi Trailanga Swami to the proper and significant upbringing and building of a great life!

We are confident that the real devotees and seekers can realise the significance of such a great life and thus the laying of solid foundation of spiritualism. We further hope that our readers living their own material lives are also able to understand these messages from this humble pen, and hopefully they will feel inspired to live pious lives by the blessings of the benevolent God.

This is a humble aspiration which the present author has been cherishing in his mind always, since years. Life will be meaningful if you always remember and honor the proverb "*Guru Kreedahi Kevalam*" (It is only the grace of the Guru that really matters).

In The Lap Of The Himalayas

All of our readers are aware of the great mountain range at the north of India that is world famous and known as 'The Himalayas'. The entire range is perpetually snow-capped and the name 'Himalaya' signifies the mountain range as the abode of snow. The word 'Himalaya' is derived from the combination of the words *'Him'* and *'Aalaya'* and thus 'Himalaya', the abode of eternal snow.

Since time immemorial, it has been famous as the most beautiful field of tranquility, providing unlimited possibilities for spiritual pursuits and meditation completely undisturbed! It is hard to estimate how many secret spiritual aspirants haved breathed their last in these mountain ranges. The spiritual vibrations from the incessant austereties of these great lives have spread over through the land, water, air, and sky and mixed in the dust particles everywhere in the world.

Such an influence of spiritual activities is rare and not available in any other human habitat other than in India. The fortunate souls who are born and brought up in this holy land can realise the greatest Eternal Truth and the Abode of Truth can become visible to their eyes. And that Truth illuminates in these mountains. Otherwise the greatest realisation that "*Sarvam Khalvidam Brahma*" (God is Omnipresent) wouldn't have been possible. The land where the *rishis*, yogis, numerous sages, ascetics and devotees have always been absorbed in their spiritual practices to reach God since time immemorial is called Bharat (India), and this land with profound holiness is referred to as 'Bharatvarsh'.

Wanderers and visitors from any country to this magnificient place full of divinity on earth, rich with sacred history cannot help but be amazed at the wealth of spirituality in here. The nature there must remind them of *Amardham* (Abode of deities) and also its Creator, as well as the origin of their ownselves too, the many auspicious moments of their lives that in turn reveal the greatness of the Omnipresent Super Consciousness.

For this reason the wise men of the past have recommended and stressed the importance of pilgrimages to shrines. This vast land of spiritual activities that has led to India being extolled as the abode of the perpetual spiritual wealth reveals this fact as the eternal religion on Indian soil.

The great *rishis* and *munis,* (the seers of the Vedic Scriptures), through their own spiritual practices, attained *'Amrita'* (the divine nectar of immortality) and affectionately addressed the entire human race as the

"Sons of the Immortal and Eternal Soul", "*Shrinvantu Vishwe Amritasya Putra Let all of you attain His grace of immortality! All the confusions, malice, violence, all the human ailments, birth, death, disease that agitate your minds will be extinct. Do not be at a loss; seek great blessings and well wishes that are ever flowing and which will enable you all to raise and awaken you to the highest planes of consciousness and thus bestow immortality to you!*

Thus, we are ever grateful to those immortal souls and pathfinders to the Kingdom of God that were these holy sages behind the Vedic Scriptures.

The highest mountain range at the north of Indian teritory is called as 'Uttarakhand'—the words '*Uttar* '(north) + '*Khand'* (part) when conjunct reads as 'Uttarakhand'. This vast tract of land has been marked by five (5) parts known as '*Pancha Dham'* (Five abodes) to enable the act of reverential circumambulation of this stretch of land. There are still immensely powerful spiritual beings that exist in these places, visible to a few elevated spiritual souls but invisible to the majority. Among them each and every being possesses divine powers and are called as *Dev* (God) or *Devi* (Goddess), and are deities that are widely worshiped everywhere.

However, let's list out the *Dhams* around Uttarakhand:–

1) The Holy Shri Kedarnath Dham

2) The Holy Shri Badrinarayan Dham or Badreekashram

3) The Holy Gomukhi or Gangotri (The origin of the Ganges)

4) The Holy Yamunotri, and

5) The Holy Manasarovar Dham (Tibet)

On *Baisakhi Sankranti* (The last day of the Bengali month Baisakhi around March–April) when Shri Shri Shankari Mataji was 24 years old, Baba Trailanga Swami initiated her with a prayer. He made her perform '*Viraja Homa'* (A fire ritual where a monk takes up the vows of renunciation, part of *sanyasa deeksha*) offering the *sutras* (aphorisms of the members) of *Brahmacharya* into the holy fire.

Afterwords she was instructed by her Gurudev to relocate to the serene solitude of the Himalayas, far away from the maddening crowds of a city and dedicate her activities to divine contemplation. Mataji, being at a tender age, naturally became a bit afraid especially since she was inexperienced in worldly matters and so she asked her Guru, "*Baba! How can I live in the Himalayas completely alone?*"

The great Guru assured her and informed that a fellow *sadhak* Shri Bholananda, who was like an elder brother to her, would accompany her and look after everything. Further, he said, "*You will even see me there at times.*" Assured by his sweet soothing words, Shri Shankari Mataji became inspired and very glad. Without any further hesitation she got ready for leaving for the vast Himalayas, showing due respect to her Guru's advice. In 1851, after bowing down and touching the feet of her Guru and her mother with her forehead, Shankari Mataji set out for the tranquil refuge of the great mountain.

She reached her destination after starting from Kashi and going via Haridwar. She achieved further spiritual success in her life as an ascetic by visiting the previously mentioned *Pancha Dham* and other important piligrimage places during her long 18 years of sojourn in the Himalayas.

Shri Shri Shankari Mataji stayed at a beautiful place, Chandra Puri, on her way to the holy Kedardham, and underwent spiritual austerities there for a considerable period of time. Then she stayed at Gupta Kashi and'Triyogi Narayan hill area for a long time—as per legend this was the place where the holy marriage of the princess Gouri Devi, the daughter of the Royal Highness of the Himalayas, the Monarch of mountains took place. The bridegroom was the Lord Shiva Himself, clad in tiger's sikn. The holy marriage was pre-ordained by the Gods. The sacrificial fire that was lit on that auspicious occasion is supposed to be still burning till date and remains so since ages.

The holy Kedarnath Dham is likewise a lofty snow capped mountain, as towering as the Dhaulagiri. The beauty of this place is incredible, like a mass of silver drawing the attention of the eyes of the visitors to its brilliance. Even during the summer, the temple of the holy Kedarnath, the local market, rooftops of houses, roads remain covered with snow. Rice or pulses cannot be properly boiled here due to excessive cold. The road approach of about 3 to 4 miles remains covered with snow.

One has to walk through the mass of snow using long solid sticks (with sharp iron shoes at the bottom) for support, which are typically used in trekking in hilly areas. Those who walk through this path are required to use shoes; however, many Hindu-widows do not wear shoes due to their blind beliefs, and thus have to suffer badly from frost bite and blisters. During winter the mass of accumulated snow reaches upto the waist of a full grown man.

Mataji used to stay in Kedardham for six months at a stretch, i.e from Bengali month of *Vaisakh* to *Ashwin*. From the month of Ashwin onwards, during the winter, the Kedarnath temple remains closed due to exessive snow-fall and the cold. During that period Mataji used to stay at Gupta Kashi, situated downhill at a lower altitude. She thus passed nine long years of unbroken spiritual practices and austerities, and in that period she stayed in different places like Kedarnath, Gangotri, Yamunotri, Utttarkashi etc.. Later on she went from Kedardham to the holy Badrikashram at Badrinarayan Dham.

Legend has it that one has to climb up and pass over the equivalent of one lakh, twenty-five thousands hills to reach Badrikashram from Haridwar! In life also, it is clearly evident that one has to face ups and downs and overcome them with determination to reach the goal of life! It is beyond a doubt that only sincere perseverance can help one be successful in any sphere of life. Now remember the kindness of the Creator of the world!

It is as if only for the comfort and safety of the health of the pilgrims and the climbers that the Creator made some hot springs near this place, which are filled with lukewarm water that comforts and invigorates the pilgrim; so that after having bathed they can go and see the *moorthy* of Badrinarayan in the temple with a joyous heart and enjoy immense pleasure having seen the much desired sight of the Great Lord! They forget their problems, whether they are physical or mental, and whatever else may come in the future.

The cold here is less compared to Kedardham during the summer. Except for the roads, this place does not get that much snow like Kedardham during the summer though it is indeed biting cold here during the winter. Mataji went up the snow covered mountain peak for a further twenty miles up from this location, to continue her spiritual practices and divine contemplation. Legend has it that Dharma Raja Yudishthira (the eldest of the Pandavas from the epic Mahabharata) climbed up to the heavens starting from that very altitude.

Mataji used to perform spiritual practices and austerities staying at the Badrinarayan Dham from the months of Vaisakh to Ashwin, a stretch of six months, and then owing to heavy snowfall, descend down the mountains reaching Joshi Math (abbotage) or Jyotir Math, covering the path traveling for four days at a stretch. After that her place for further spiritual practices for next six months would be at even lower places at Vash Ashram etc.

1) Joshi Math — in the north Himalayas. Joshi Math is the first *math* establish by Shri Adi Shankaracharya.

2) Shringeri Math — in present day Karnataka

3) Govardhan Math — at Puri Dham and Jagannath-Dham, considered to be the abode of Lord Jagannath.

4) Sharada Math — at Dwaraka-dham.

Mataji also did intense spiritual practices at the place that is famous and is known as Manasarovar situated in Tibet, for a considerable span of time. The holy Kailash Parvat (Peak) is situated just above the Manasarovar. By the grace of her spiritual father and guide Baba Trailanga Swami, she went to Kailash and then upto the holy mount Meru (the North Pole), the solar regions, the lunar regions, and the planet Mars in her subtle spiritual body.

She passed a long period of time in meditation, starting at the Vyasa Guha (Cave of Vyasa) on the banks of Vyasa Kunda (the lake named after Maharishi Veda Vyasa) situated at the foothills of the Kailash Mountain. She had the rare fortune of seeing Devi Bhagavati Herself (The Goddess Bhagavati is considered to be the source of all Shakti in the universe) face to face and that wonderful experience wiped off all her remaining doubts and confusions for ever.

She reached her final accomplishment as an ascetic, having comprehended all the aspects of the visible or invisible, of God with form or formless. Henceforth she had been living a full existence with complete knowledge of the *Poorna Brahma* (Supreme Consciousness of God).

Chamree cows (the yaks) are found in the higher regions of the mountains and in Tibet in quite some numbers. Milk from their udders is often seen oozing spontaneously. The sages and other spiritual seekers collect the condensed mass of yak milk that has been spontaneously spilled and has become frozen from wherever they can find it.

They collect it and drink this extremely nutritious and sweet milk by melting the frozen mass with the heat of a fire. A lesser known brethren of the yak that is often seen here is called 'Jhabbu'. It is covered with thick bushy hair and the Tibeteans use it for carrying loads. Bholanandaji, the *gurubhai* (brother-disciple to the same Guru) to Mataji also used to collect wild-fruits or hill radishes for Mataji as her food. She accepted them as her food without any hesitation.

Often, she used to eat some kind of locally available leaves having roasted in fire which produced the same taste as bread! Besides, Baba Trailanga Swami used to go to Mataji's place in his subtle body to supply a special kind of 'snow-fruit' to his favourite disciple. The fruit had a special characteristic; one who takes the special 'snow-fruit' does not feel hunger or thirst for six months! Eating ripe yellow myrobalans also results in the same effect. In the lower plains, ripe myrobalans are very hard to find, and even when someone finds it, it is usually offered to the deities.

Owing to a shortage, ripe myrobalans are unlikely to be found. After eating this invigorating fruit Mataji would not consume any other food for six long months. She would take her seat for long six months while meditating deeply, without the need to even urinate or evacuate bowels. The holy Trailanga Swami was, as if, at the beck and call of his dear disciple; whenever Mataji remembered him he used to appear before her eyes as the living form of divine blessings!

Return of Mataji from the Himalayas

The retreat ended. Her Holiness Shri Shri Shankari Mataji, the celibate ascetic, returned to her childhood abode, the holy Kashidham, after long 18 years of solitary life in the lap of the Himalayas. In the serene calm of the great mountain she had passed her days as a practioner of *Raja Yoga* (Balanced Path of Yoga) and made great spiritual progress. Now she was coming back to Kashidham and returning to the feet of her Guru accompanied by her Gurubhai Bholanathji in the year 1869 at the age of 42 years.

In all this while, she had come downhill only once following some unspoken command from her Guru Trailanga Swami and reached Prayag in Allahabad, and stayed there for 30 days when she was 30 years old. That was the time when Sepoy-mutiny was happening against the British rule. She had left for the Himalayas via the holy Vrindavan, a deeply significant piligrimage place in the context of the religious history of India.

The day when Shri Shri Shankari Mataji left for solitude and the life of deep meditation in the tranquility of the Himalayas, she had only one sari which she was wearing, with the second one left behind by her left out to dry under the sun, in the verandah of the ashram. Coming back to the ashram, when she went to meet her own mother, she was astounded on seeing the sari that she had left behind out to dry, exactly as it was when she left.

Out of her deep love for her darling daughter, who was living far away, Shri Shri Shankari Mataji's mother would not move the sari, as it was a token of the memory of her dear daughter. Shri Shri Shankari Mataji would never stop herself from shedding tears whenever she described that incident. What an instance of fathomless motherly love! Let all the motherhood of the world be respected by us and let all of us all over the world worship our mothers, who represent the Original Mother of the universe!!

For such a long period of time Ambalika Devi, her mother, had never got the opportunity to see her, and because of this reason she could not recognise her own daughter who had the look of a veteran renunciate , complete with thick matted hair.

Overwhelmed at the sight of a renunciate, she was even about to touch the feet of her daughter whom she considered to be a representation of the Eternal Mother, Jagadamba, the Mother of the universe. Another reason behind her confusion was that in her childhood Mataji was thin and slender bodied, but after 18 years she had put on weight and that decieved the eyes of her mother. But on Shankari Mataji's part, she was able to recognise her mother at the first sight.

She said to her mother, *"Maa, don't you recognise me. I am your own daughter, Shankari."* Now we leave it up to the reader's internal eyes! Just imagine the unspeakable emotions in that reunion of a mother with her child and realise the depth of their happiness!!

After some days Shri Shri Shankari Mataji suddenly got a thought that she had not been able to worship Lord Vishwanath for a long period of time.

One day she started for the temple of Lord Vishwanath with some tender green-leaves of the fruit named as *Bilva* marmelos (wood apple) and flowers for worshiping the Lord of the universe. All of a suddent another thought appeared in her mind that "Baba Trailanga Swamiji is none other than Lord Viswanath Himself!"

But her mind was still not decided. She went to the temple, and worshiped the idol of Lord Viswanath there. Returning back to ashram she was utterly astounded to see that the flowers and the *Bilva* leaves that she had placed over the head of the idol of the Lord Shiva after offering her prayers were seen on the head of Baba Trailanga Swami, who was deeply absorbed in meditation.

Since then all her doubts disappeared from her mind forever. She became firm in her belief that Trailanga Swami was none other than the Holiness Lord Shiva Himself; at the same time she was immensely happy knowing that she had the rare fortune to have such a great Guru's graceful affection.

We feel that in this context we should remember the wise opinions from another great saint, Shri Ramakrishna Paramahamsa. Swami Saradanandaji, a direct disciple to Shri Ramakrishna Paramahamsa wrote:

"Thakur Shri Ramakrishna Dev met all the famous saints of Kashi during his stay there in Kashi. Among them all Baba Trailanga Swami influenced him highly and he felt attracted to him. He used to mention many things about Trailanga Swami to us. He said, "I saw the manifestation of the holy Lord Viswanath in Trailanga Swami. He was in the state of true knowledge. He was completely detached from his own physical state. When under the heat of the sun, the sand was too hot to even walk on, Trailanga Swami would be seen lying on the hot sand." Cooking a pudding made of milk, rice, and sugar, Paramahamsa Dev went to him and fed him with the preparation. He was in his vow of silence at that time. Shri Ramakrishna asked him by gestures of his fingers whether God is One or many. He also replied by gestures that when you are in the reality of the mundane, God is many; when you are deeply merged in meditation God is absolutely One."

(Shri Shri Ramakrishna Leela Prasanga—Part 4)

Shri Shri Shankari Mataji was living in the underground chamber—(the previously mentioned chamber under the altar of Swami Trailanga Swami—which was used as the room for meditation) after returning back from the Himalayas, when Shri Ramakrishna Paramahamsa went to the ashram of Trailanga Swami.

Following the gestures from Trailanga Swami, his direct disciple and *gurubhai* of Shri Shri Shankari Mataji, Mangal Bhattji entered the underground chamber and told her, "A Bengali sage has arrived. Baba has asked you to come up!" Mataji came up the stairs and saw a very fair complexioned Bengali *Paramhansa* with *tejas* (divine brilliance) conversing with Trailanga Swami.

He was accompained by a Bengali gentleman with a '*shamla*' (a special kind of turban used by the Bengali aristocrats of that age) on his head. Later on she came to know that he was the well-known Mathur Nath Biswas, who was the son-in-law of Rani Rashmoni, the founder of the world famous temple at Dakshineswar. Shri Shri Shankari Mataji could understand a few significant words and sentences of the conversation bewteen Ramkrishna Dev and Trailanga Swami. We are quoting a few of them –

1) Paramahamsadev — "Is God an Absolute One, or many?"

Trailanga Swami — He is only One when the ascetic is in the deep of his meditation completely removed from the mundane. That is called the *Advaitavad* (the concept of monotheism). When the fervent search and devotion of a devotee reaches the zenith of his quest, at that point He is Two. That is to say one part is the devotee himself and the other part is God: This is called the doctrine of Dualism (the *Dvaitavad*)

So, you can opine that God is One and Two, but actually he is One — the Absolute. The two parts of beads making a chick-pea, is the perfect example of this concept.

2) Paramahamsadev — What do you mean by 'religion' (*dharma*)?

Trailanga Swami — Truth (*satya*)

3) Paramahamsadev — What is the real duty (*karma*) of a man?

Trailanga Swami — Service to all beings. (*Jiv Seva*) He prays best who loves best all things both great and small.

4) Paramahamsadev — What is love? (*prem*)

Trailanga Swami — When tears flow in the eyes of a devout man while taking the name of God, that is love.

Hearing such concise but indisputable and moving replies from Trailanga Swamiji, Shri Shri Ramakrishna Paramahamsa Dev was immediately moved into a mystical state contemplating God.

Tears of love for God rolled down his cheek—stream of pearls flooded down his chin through the outer canthus of his eyes. We would like to remind you that tears coming out from the inner canthus of eyes and by the side of the nose are considered to be a sign of grief—the tears of lamentation. Shri Trailanga Swami suggested Mataji to fan Shri Ramakrishna Paramahamsadev with a fan made from the leaves of the palm trees.

When Ramakrishna Paramahamsadev was back from his trance (*Bhava Samadhi*), he began to lift his hands up and dance encircling the altar of Trailanga Swami. Later on he fetched 20 seers of milk pudding and fed Trailanga Swami with his own hands.

Both of them began to float on sea of love for God. They talked to each other about spiritual topics during their full union of the hearts, but those were beyond the realisation of others present there. This inner state of mind is the Kingdom of God. This is the real state of heart and soul that can be termed as '*Swarajya Dharma*' or '*Swadharma*' (The own and independent abode of the inner self).

When one reaches that state, all of one's duties are performed perfectly in their true sense. Everything merges into the state of divine bliss, and the fullest assimilation of the devotee's soul takes place and the merger brings complete peace of mind and soul. These holy souls in turn can bring peace all over the world and carry the torch of spiritualism for ailing mankind.

The Kingdom of God is the true kingdom of religion and peace—immaculate, unstained and absolute. No petty differences of jealousy, malice, quarrels, big or small, rich or pauper exist here in this Kindgom of Heaven. Where such petty differences are extinct, only there is the establishment of the Kingdom of God possible. This is the essence of our eternal religion and it is absolutely perpetually true.

"*Man jeete to jagat jeete*"— If one conquers one's innate nature, then one has conquered the world. The Supreme Truth—the Almighty can be comprehended only by unstained souls. Therefore, first and foremost, reaching the Divine is possible only when the soul of man cherishes piousness and avoids useless wishes and missions. It is not difficult for such clean souls to realise the greatest of all knowledge.

Just imagine—what fantastic spiritual union it must have been, an incredible place where they were deeply absorbed in the ceaseless bliss of the Divine! On one hand there is Trailanga Swami—the soul with deep understanding of all the scriptures, unrivalled master of all the doctrines on spiritual truths, and on the other hand the almost illiterate but full of the divine realisation, one who has realised the greatest essence of all the doctrines of all major religons, the true lover of God and unstained soul—Shri Shri Ramakrishna Paramahamsa Dev! Both of them were completely absorbed in the thought and quest for God, the Supreme Almighty!

॥ ॐ तत् सत् ॥

|| om tat sat ||

Appendix A: Humble Request to Readers

We have the aspiration of further taking this narrative to the post Himalayan life and spiritual journey of Shri Shri Mataji, along with all the other significant incidents that took place after the meeting between Shri Ramakrishna Paramahamsadev and Trailanga Swami including the descriptions of her tours and visits in many others places, in the later editions of this book. Up to the year 1932, our beloved spiritual mother Shri Shri Shankari Mataji traveled all over the Indian Territory on pilgrimages of significance, as a female renunciate with the grace of her Guru Trailanga Swamiji.

It was the 20th of the month of *Asadh* (July 3, 1931), when by the grace of God the humble author of this book had the good fortune of meeting her holiness Shri Shri Shankari Mataji at Darjeeling hill station in the lap of the Himalayas.

The author was also traveling alone over many places and pilgrimage destinations when he had the significant fortune to see his spiritual mother for the first time. In the cremation ground of Darjieeling, Mataji could see the '*Vishwaroop*' (All prevading omnipresent form) of Mahaswami with her company of disciples. In those days, owing to the fervent wishes and prayer, the arrival of the holy sage Trailanga Swami in the midst of the mass of clouds was visible to them clearly and they became elated and immensely overjoyed by the divine sight.

The author also had the good fortune of meeting the celebrated disciples of some great sages during his life employed in service, and thereafter during his travels. However, there was still an eager unsatiated desire in him to know that if there were any of the female disciples of Baba Trailanga Swami of the holy Kashi-dham that were still alive.

I had a keen desire also to meet her in case she was still living. I found out that Shri Shri Shankari Mata was still living. I prayed to God with sincerity and made a heartfelt appeal and the *Kalpataru* (the compassionable God who is like the wish-fulfilling tree) favoured me with his grace and fulfilled my wishes.

Then on hearing the detailed description of the celebrated pilgrimage destination 'Parashuram Tirtha' located at the north-eastern border area in Assam, I felt an earnest desire to visit the place. Later, after some days spent in humble service to my spiritual mother and in her proximity, I went to Assam and visited all the pilgrimage centres of reputation and met the celebrated residents including the holy Parashuram Tirtha and saw the holy 'Govindji' (another name of Lord Krishna). Then having completed my long journey, I returned to the residence of Babu Manomohan Ghosh, superintendent of polytechnical school, at 66, Baghbazar Street, Kolkata 700003, following the order and advice of Shri Shri Shankari Mataji.

Since then the humble author of this book has had the great fortune to be at the lotus feet of Shri Shri Shankari Mataji as a humble servant. Afterwords I accompanied Mataji to visit the *Kumbha Mela* in Nashik, Maharashtra, Gomti Dwarka and finally to Bet Dwarka.

There I got a severe case of pneumonia, but by the kind grace and tireless care of my spiritual mother, I came round after a few days. It was almost like a revival leading to a new life. Next we went to Karachi via the port of Okha. Immediately after the visit to Karachi, we went to the Narayan Sarovar (a holy lake named after 'Narayan' — the manifestation of Lord Vishnu) by a ship.

The lake is situated in the free land of Kaccha, where on the 27th day of the month of *Kartik* (November 14, 1932), I had the invaluable fortune of being initiated with *mantra deeksha* from the ever merciful spiritual mother Shri Shri Shankari Mataji. Since then I have been living at her holy feet as a humble servant and thus passing my life in spiritual practices, named as 'Paramananda Saraswati'. All right, there you have it, my dear reader!! Let all of us strive for the re-establishment of Truth, in these days of chaos prevailing all over the world.

"Trailanga Manasaje Mahayog Siddhe Sakshat Sadashiv Sneha Samriddhe.
Swadhyay Parayane Satata Dhyanasthe Namo Namo "Shankari" Jananee
Namoh Stuteh"

The First Edition Concludes

Appendix B: The Virgin Saint

Extract from an article "The Kumbha Mela"—India's world famous Assembly of Saints—held in Haridwar, in March 1938. By Premananda Brahmachari (Now Srimat Swami Binoyananda Giri—in charge, Jogada Math, Dakshineshwar, Calcutta.) in the November Issue of 'Inner Culture', 1938, Organ of the Self Realisation Fellowship Church Ire, 3880 San Rafael Avenue, Los Angeles, California, America.

Woman (Virgin) Saint of 112 Years

"We went to see the great Shankari Matajiew. She is a disciple, the only living disciple of the late Trailanga Swami, the most illustrious yogi of Benares (U.P).

I had heard about her two years before and eagerly longed to see her once. Fortunately she went to Haridwar during the Kumbh Mela, where I had the proud privilege of meeting her for the first time.

Her age is now 112 years...She was born in Benares, in March 1827, being the daughter of one of the disciples of Trailanga Swami. She is unmarried, having been trained & initiated by Trailanga Swami from her very childhood. She is an expounder of *Raja Yoga* (the Kingly Yoga or Balanced Path) and said that she had met Yogavatar Lahiri Maharaj (the Master of Swami Sri Yukteshwar Giriji) in Benares in an ecstatic condition under a tree & surrounded by several disciples. I was very happy to get her pictures, taken on the bank of the holy Ganges."

Tales of her training

"I was fascinated by her face beaming with purity and intelligence of a very fine type (*sathwle*). Though enjoying a ripe old age of more than a century, her body seems to have defied the rigours of age. Decrepitude could not attack her body. Her hair is black, complexion bright, body quite fit to outwit the ravages of time for many years to come. Her conversations charmed me. I frequented her place often. She described to me the systematic training she had to undergo as a *brahmacharini* 'woman-ascetic' at the age of 12 in a small cave underneath the seat of her Guru for twelve years at Benares; at at the age of 24 she was given *sanyas* and was asked to meditate for perfect realization in the Himalayas—for which she spent 18 years in Kedarnath, Gongotri,

Jamunotri; Badrinath, Sat-path; Koilas and Manas-Sarobor. After 1888 she made her travels all over India—visiting Kabul, Ceylon, Dwaraka, Karachi-Narayan Sarobor, Amarnath-Sarada Pith (Kashmir), Manipur, Burma, and Pashupatinath, etc. I heard her descriptions with rapt attention, realizing how fortunate she was to have the privilege of the personal touch of such a great yogi."

Astonishing Disappearance of the Great Saint Trailanga Swamiji's body

She said that her Guru was still living and that he meets her when necessary to solve some knotty problems, and helps her in all the other possible ways. She said that the dead body of her Guru had vanished from the stone box, where it has been kept for immersion in the Ganges, according to the last wish of Trailanga Swami. (This incident is similar to that of Kabir—a great Indian monk).

But the disappearance of the dead body of Trailanga Swami had been so long unknown to the general public. This is the first time that I had come to know it as it is not even mentioned in the 'Life of Trailanga Swami', written by Mr. Umacharan Mukherjee.

Shankari Mai, in my opinion, is not a follower of Bhakti Yoga, but is trying to *solve the problem of life through a complete surrender of the self to the Guru*, not blindly but with a rationalistic analysis of the problem of our lives in its various aspects, believing that "Religion is an Individual Problem".

The complete translation of the above extract has been printed in our "Nityo Puja Paddhati" (Methods of regular prayer and worship) by Swami Paramananda Saraswati.

Appendix C—From a Journal in the UK

Extract from an article titled "India To-morrow" published in the Strand Magazine, January 1937, written by the famous English writer, Mr. F. Yeats Brown, after we had met each other in the Prayag Kumbha Mela, held in Jan. 1936

"Freaks are great fun and far more popular with the crowd than the 'Philosophers' I have come to seek. Amongst the latter the most remarkable is Her Holiness Sankari Ma, a virgin saint reputed to be one hundred and nine years old... 'Long life is a question of internal purity', she tells me, 'and of right repose. Most of us sleep too much and carelessly. We should learn how to relax properly. We can decide for ourselves when we want to die, save for accidents. I hope to live 180 years. My Teacher, Trailanga Swamiji, practiced yoga in the Himalayas and he lived for about 300 years. He took his last *samadhi*, in December, 1887, in Benares.'"

"At present she has only one *sanyasi* follower, a middle aged retired doctor (now Swami Paramananda Saraswati) who speaks perfect English."

... "When I take my leave I ask him whether I may make her a small present, for I know that this other-worldly couple is entirely dependent on charity for their food."

"Certainly", he answers, "you may put a coin upon Holy Mother's toe." "I do,—as I am told. Her Holiness hardly notices the rupee, for her mind is already fixed on the beautitudes beyond this world."[2]

(Abridged).

---

[2] The translation of the original Bengali manuscript ends here

Epilogue

The second edition mentioned by Swami Paramanda in Appendix A could never come out after Mataji's death in 1949. Here is a short summary of some of the facts which have come to light through the extensive research conducted by the publisher.

Shankari Ma traveled extensively after the *Mahasamadhi* of the Mahaguru. In 1931, an extraordinary event took place. Mataji performed a *Maha Yagya* of 45 days in the cremation ground of Darjeeling to obtain a *darshan* of Trailanga Swami for all her assembled disciples. On the concluding day of the *Maha Yagya*, July 3, 1932, which fell on the Vijaya Dashami day at the end of the Maha Navaratri Puja, the Mahaswami blessed them by clearly appearing in the midst of the mass of clouds. This extraordinary event was witnessed by many. This *Vishwaroop Darshan* left everyone elated and speechless.

There was another enactment of his appearance at Madurai on October 9, 1932. There also, after Mataji's *sankalp* and *Maha Yagya* and the fervent prayers of the assembled North Indian *bairagi* sadhus and *sanyasis*, Trailanga Swami granted them his *darshan* by emerging out of the Samadhi Cave. His divine form was fully covered with *Vibhuti* (sacred ash).

Mataji finally settled at Kashi around 1940 and established a 'Bhajan Ashram' at Aundh Garbi in Harish Chandra Ghat. This is the place where this biography was discovered by the publisher in 2007. This was the place where the great woman ascetic consciously left her mortal body on March 1, 1949 (at half past midnight) at the grand age of 122 years.

There was another notable disciple of Shankari Ma – Swami Raman Giri. A Swedish aristocrat, he relinquished great wealth and came to Benaras Hindu University on a two year scholarship to study religious and philosophical yore. His original name was Per Westin. He was born on June 19, 1921 in Sweden. On being told that theoretical knowledge was not enough and if he wanted to realize the truth, he had to find a realized master who could teach him, he came to Mataji who initiated him into Raja Yoga by touching his head. She lovingly blessed him

Swami Raman Giri

and purified his body and mind by transmitting her yogic power into his soul.

It was his intense love for his guru mother which brought him to be present with her on the last day of her life in the mortal world. It was the day of Holi, the Hindu festival of colors – February 28, 1949. He had the great fortune to partake the food prepared and served by her own hands on the same day. It was he who took the last photograph of Shankari Ma with Swami Paramananda Saraswati on the rooftop of 'Bhajan Ashram' on that fateful day.

After the *Mahasamadhi* of Mataji, he moved down south to Madurai in April 1949. He met Ramana Maharashi and was given the name 'Raman Giri'. He established his ashram in a hilly region, close to the birth place of Trailanga Swami, adjacent to the first Samadhi Temple of Trailanga Swami. Here he continued his *sadhana* and attained perfection. He passed away at the young age of thirty-four, in 1955. As a true and perfect yogi, he left his mortal body seated in true yogic fashion, through the small hole in his skull, *Brahmarandhra*. His body was interred at the foot of Sirumalai Hills, at a place he had named 'Raman Padam', and a *Shivalinga* was installed over his *Samadhi*.

A Note from the Editor

I must confess that I am quite reluctant to insert any reference to me in the pages of this holy book. I am doing so purely deferring to the wishes of Shri Amarnathji Poddar. Quite simply, I felt extremely unqualified for the task of editing this book. My sincere apologies for any mistakes made by me in this effort, I tried to help to the best of my limited abilities, and as an offering to the divine feet of the Mahaswami

॥ सर्वम् श्री कृष्णार्पणमस्तु ॥

And I would like to make a couple of comments for the benefit of the readers, to help them follow the flow better:

- You might have come across repetitions of stories and incidents, and digressions from the main narrative. Readers should keep in mind that this book is a compilation of a series of discourses by Shri Shri Shankari Mataji, which the author tried to capture verbatim, and also conveys the wisdom of his own experiences.

- In many places, while editing, I preferred to let the words of the author prevail over grammatical correctness. Changing too much could have potentially altered what the author was trying to convey.

I would also like to place on record my deep gratitude to Shri P.V.R. Narasimha Rao, a Sanskrit scholar and noted astrologer based in Boston, for rendering Shri Trailangashtakam in Devanagari for this book, and to my brother Raj, who skillfully did the final round of editing, and touching up of the content in this book.

Dinesh N.

Acknowledgements

The noble folks without whose sincere help and inspiration this invaluable book would not have been published must be mentioned here.

Prominent among them are Shri Jagat Jyoti Chowdhury , Shri Debasish Mukherjee , Shri Tapash Chakraborty (Ret Judge), Shrimati Chameli Das, Kalpana Sengupta & Kamala Sen , and Abhoy Sarkar Vice President of Shri Guru Ashram Trailanga Math. Shri Dinesh N, based in California, a devotee of Mahatma Trailanga Swami, took this divine & rare opportunity to edit and present this English Version of the book appropriately, including providing the Sanskrit text & *shlokas* in Devanagari script as found in the original Bengali book on *Parivrajaka* Shri Shankari Mataji. The non-Bengali & non-Hindi knowing multitudes of Mahaswamiji's devotees all over the globe are indebted to, and ever remember, Shri Dinesh N. for his noble effort of editing this hitherto unknown rare book on the *Manasa Putri* of Mahatma Shri Shri Trailinga Swamiji. Acknowledging his dedication, I pray to the Mahaguru to continue to shower his blessings on this noble grandson and devotee.

Last but not the least, may the Mahaguru bless Prachi Jawlekar and Bhushan Jawlekar, who took the initiative in publishing the book for the benefit of readers and devotees across the world.

If there are any unintended mistakes despite my best efforts, the readers are requested to kindly forgive it out of their benevolence and grace. I shall also be deeply obliged if any additional details are sent to me by anybody who knows more about the Mahaguru and Shri Mataji. This book is published bearing the blessings of Yogeshwar Bhagavan Shri Shri Trailanga Swamiji Maharaj and His disciple Maha Yogini Shri Shri Shankari Mataji.

Amarnath Poddar

Glossary

Translations that have been omitted are listed out herre

1. "*Sab Debatake Pujan Kori Istha Dev Ke Bhajan Kori* "— I worship all the deities and pray to my choosen deity)
2. "*Tanhar (Swamijir) Nikat Dikkhito Hoibo Bhabiya Jeevanke Dhonyo Mone Korilam*" — I considered my life successful in the thought that I would be given *mantra deeksha* the next day.
3. "*Agamee Kalyo Diksha Diben Boliyachen*"— He assured that he would provide and bless me with the *mantra deeksha* tomorrow"
4. "*Ami Shayan Korite Pari*" — I can lie down
5. "*Upabeshan Korite Pari*" — I can sit too
6. "*Bedeer Pashe*" — Beside the altar
7. "*Bedeer Nimne*" — Under the altar
8. "*Tanhake Sinduker Bhitar Bhalo Bichanay Shayan Karaiya*" — Having laid him on a comfortable bed inside the chest
9. "*Ei Sakal Ghatanay Jaha Dekhile Ebong Sei Sakal Katabarta Jaha Sunile Abishwasi Loker Nikat Boliyo Naa*" — The incidents that you witnessed and the conversations you heard, do not express or reveal them to anybody who does not believe in such incidents
10. "*Hridoy Bidirno Hoite Lagilo, Dukkhe Buk Fatiya Jaite Lagilo, Eto Diner Par Ami Bal Buddhi Sakoli Jahakichu Sakoli Harailam*" — My heart was breaking, a sense of profound grief was almost tearing my heart, after a long time. I had lost all my mental strength and fortitude
11. "*Inhar Bibaha Korite Adou Ichha Chilona, Kebal Matar Anurodhe Bibaha Koriya Chilen*" — He had no intention at all to marry. But at last he agreed to live a married life to abide by his mother's request
12. "*Rogee Bhogee Yogee Aankhse Nishan Aur Aankh Se Pehchan*" — A patient (a man suffering from any disease), a hedonist, and a man of pious nature can all be identified by their eyes, as their innerselves are reflected in their eyes

13. "*Jukta Yogi Trailanga Swami*" — Trailanga Swami, the Liberated Yogi

14. "*Swadeshe Pujyate Raja Bidyan Sarbatra Pujyate*" — A king is worshiped within his own kingdom, whereas a man of wisdom is worshiped and respected all over the world

15. "*Jukto Yogee*" — Liberated Yogi

16. "*A Jagate Keu Karo Shatru Mitra Noy, Byabohare Shatru Mitro Porichoy Hoy*" — Identifying who is a friend and who is a foe depends on observing their behaviour, manners. Otherwise there is no way to to judge a friend from a foe.

17. "*Antare For Dyakh Cheye Setha Ananda Niketan*" — Look at your inner self and realise that you are immensely wealthy in the core of your heart, and with the grace of God, you do not need anything to long for as you are divinely booned

18. "*Bhalo Aasane Bosaiya*" — Setting him in sitting position on a comfortable seat

19. "*Bichanay*" — in the bed

20. "*Shayan Karaiya*" — Laying him down

21. "*Ami Panchti Sishya Koriyachi*" — I have given *mantra deeksha* to five disciples

Made in the USA
Middletown, DE
06 May 2025

75223351R00099